ISBN 978-1-331-66266-2
PIBN 10219542

E MINISTRY OF ABSOLUTION

THE MINISTRY OF ABSOLUTION

AN APPEAL FOR ITS MORE GENERAL USE WITH DUE REGARD TO THE LIBERTY OF THE INDIVIDUAL

BY

CYRIL BICKERSTETH, M.A.

OF THE COMMUNITY OF THE RESURRECTION

LONGMANS, GREEN AND CO.

39 PATERNOSTER ROW, LONDON

NEW YORK, BOMBAY, AND CALCUTTA

1912

PREFACE

In order to indicate the point of view from which this little book has been written, I venture to give some extracts from two lectures delivered at Worcester in November 1898 by Dr. Charles Gore, Bishop of Oxford, who was then Canon of Westminster and Superior of the Community of the Resurrection. They are fully reported in the *Guardian* (Nov. 9 and 16, 1898). In the first Dr. Gore sketches the history of the penitential discipline of the Church at large, and throws a good deal of light on the subject discussed in Chapter XI. of this volume. In the second he speaks of the penitential discipline of the Church of England since the Reformation, with some very practical suggestions as to the duty of the clergy:—

"Our conditions are different from those of the early Church, or the mediæval Church, or the Church of the sixteenth and seventeenth centuries. How are all these principles and directions to be applied? The first point to notice is that the whole theory of Church penitential discipline implies a social view of sin. It is not merely a personal matter between the soul and God. Our private sins (so called), our lusts and selfishness . . . are wrongs to the Church, the Body, as well as offences against God, and impoverishments of our own souls. In injuring our souls we rob and injure the Church. This is the great principle, and it is the perception of this that is so lamentably lacking in ordinary English Christianity

"How are we to restore to the ordinary conscience that sense of obligation to the Church which is the moral basis of Church discipline?

"The early discipline of the Church was, we must remember, very imperfect in result, but none the less very valuable in its moral witness. . . . We must not allow the profound moral ideal of the Prayer-book and the New Testament to remain a dead letter—we are 'to judge those within.' And it must never be forgotten that the whole historical position of private confession shows it to be a preparation or a substitute for the public discipline. . . .

"The recollection of this vital principle is best secured by private confession being kept, as our Church intends, thoroughly voluntary; and that not merely in the sense in which all religious acts are worthless which do not involve an act of will. In the latter sense Communion is voluntary. Auricular confession is voluntary in the further sense that the Church requires no one to make it unless their own conscience urges them to. It is not the only method accepted by the Church of recovery from every grievous sin, but *one* method. It is our business to see that all Churchmen know of its existence and meaning.

"It may be desirable that Bishops should forbid us to begin to hear confessions, or confessions of persons of the other sex, till we are thirty years old. Anyway, we should train ourselves to be judicious confessors, with adequate moral knowledge, whenever we are called upon to exercise the ministry. The Latin Rules given as helps to hearing confession in the *Priest's Book of Private Devotion* are for the most part, I think, sensible. [A translation is given in Chapter V.] But the requisite moral knowledge is to be derived in the main from knowledge of men and women and their temptations, and (especially) from a close and constant study of the moral principles and precepts of the Bible. Mr. Ottley's essay on Christian Ethics in *Lux Mundi* may help us to study the subject. It must always be remembered that Roman books of moral theology are directed towards a system of obligatory confession, which is in some respects different not only in degree, but almost in kind, from that under which we live and work. Good sense, good feeling, and clear Christian principles are what we want to help souls.

"I cannot conclude without saying, as one who both makes and hears confessions, that, living as we do, in a self-excusing age, and surrounded as one is by too kind friends, it is a discipline of enormous moral value. Like every other good thing, it may be easily misused. It is misused when it is allowed to minister to a love of being directed from outside, instead of using one's own judgment and depending on the personal guidance of the Holy Spirit. But *abusus non tollit usum*. Confession need not mean direction, and direction may be over-much sought without confession. Confession seems to me a practice very much to be recommended to the returning penitent, and to persons in crises of their lives, as often before confirmation, or marriage, or ordination. We clergy perhaps especially need such discipline, and in many cases where people are over-much given to introspection and scrupulousness, it may be a blessed instrument of moral liberty."

I quote these words, not as claiming the approval of the Bishop for this little book, which in fact he has not read, but as showing the present attitude towards the ministry of absolution, which is I believe shared by a large, and I hope growing, body of priests in the Church of England. My only excuse for writing on a subject of exceptional difficulty is that, while I have been engaged in mission work since 1884, I have been in constant communication with many of the men who are trying to work on the lines which Bishop Gore has laid down. I owe much more than I can express to my brethren in the Community of the Resurrection; but though they have given me much generous help in the preparation of the book, they should not be held responsible for any failure on my part to express the convictions which we hold in common.

Though this book is primarily intended for the clergy, I hope there is nothing in it to offend the conscience of lay readers, who will join in the prayer that we may be efficient as "Ministers of Christ and stewards of the mysteries of GOD."

CYRIL BICKERSTETH.

CONTENTS

I

INTRODUCTION

II

CONFESSION AND LIBERTY

VI

THE ORDINARY USE OF CONFESSION

VII

PAROCHIAL MISSIONS

VIII

THE FORM OF CONFESSION

IX

ON WITHHOLDING ABSOLUTION

THE

MINISTRY OF ABSOLUTION

I

INTRODUCTION

IN the Preface to Bishop Jeremy Taylor's *Ductor Dubitantium* he remarks that there was in the Reformed Churches a great scarcity of books on cases of conscience.

"For any public provision of books of casuistical theology we were almost wholly unprovided, and like the children of Israel in the days of Saul and Jonathan we were forced to go down to the forges of the Philistines to sharpen every man his share and his coulter, his axe and his mattock. We had swords and spears of our own, enough for defence and more than enough for disputation; but in this more necessary part of the conduct of consciences we did receive our answers from abroad, till we found that our old needs were sometimes very ill supplied, and new necessities did every day arise."

A

These words were written in 1659, and it cannot be said that much has been done since by Anglican divines to roll away this reproach. Bishop Jeremy Taylor's own work remains as a monument of solid learning, but it does not seem to attract the modern reader, or to supply the needs of the young priest who looks for practical guidance in the exercise of his ministry to individual souls. It is not surprising that for nearly two hundred years after Jeremy Taylor's time little or nothing was done to supply a want which was scarcely felt. It remained the case, as Jeremy Taylor says, "that the careless and needless neglect of receiving private confesssions hath been too great a cause of our not providing materials apt for so pious and useful a ministration."

But through the mercy of God there has been during the past fifty years a real revival of penitence amongst us; and there is a great, and growing, number of faithful children of the Church in England, who expect their clergy to be not merely preachers, and organisers of public worship, but real spiritual guides and fathers in Christ. In Dr. Pusey's introduction to the Abbé Gaume's *Manual for Confessors*, published in 1877, he shows how the use of confession and the desire for absolution revived amongst us. It was not due to deliberate teaching on the part of the clergy; but when, under the influence of the Oxford Tracts, preachers began to insist on the gravity of post-baptismal sin, "it fell on people's hearts like a thunder-clap."

The practice of confession spread from conscience to conscience, before there was any oral teaching as to the remedy. Living men whose minds were stirred taught the nature of the disease: the Prayer-book which the Church of England put into the hands of all her children in their own language taught the remedy. "Without any other living teaching, men (for the enlarged use of confession began with men), men whose consciences were awakened learned to lay down the burden of their sins at our dear Lord's feet: and He by virtue of His words, 'Whose soever sins ye remit, they are remitted unto them,' said to their inmost souls, 'Thy sins be forgiven thee; go in peace.' In those stirring times, people saw the change wrought in the outward life of their acquaintance, and asked, 'What has changed you so?' The answer, 'I have been to confession,' suggested the thought, 'Then it might be good for me too.'"

Dr. Pusey's book, from which the above is quoted, was published at a time when public opinion was deeply stirred. An attempt had been made to aid the clergy in their ministry by the private circulation of a manual called the *Priest in Absolution.* Unfortunately, this book achieved an unenviable and undeserved notoriety. It was certainly not the kind of book which would have been written by Mr. Keble, Dr. Pusey himself, or by such men as George Howard Wilkinson, who was then beginning his wonderful ministry at S. Peter's, Eaton Square, and leading innumerable souls by his evangelical preaching to sacramental confession. In the judgment of the present writer it contained many disputable statements and entered into unnecessary details, appearing to encourage a wrong method of dealing with souls; but the clamour raised against it was altogether unreasonable. To make extracts from a medical journal and to proclaim them upon the housetops might well be an outrage on public decency, but the responsibility for such an outrage should rest not with the original writers, but with the unscrupulous people who spread abroad what was meant for the private information of responsible students.

Dr. Pusey's edition of the Abbé Gaume avoids the subject which roused the opponents of the *Priest in Absolution* to unmeasured fury. He omits altogether the questions on the Seventh Commandment which the Abbé Gaume says should be used under certain circumstances, in assisting an uninstructed penitent to relieve his conscience. At the time he was wise. It was important to show that the Seventh Commandment is not the one to which the mind of priest or penitent chiefly needs to be directed, and it is precisely there that great caution is needed when, as Jeremy Taylor puts it, we are driven to sharpen our weapons at the forges of the Philistines.

On the other hand, a writer who desires to help his brethren to make full proof of their ministry, cannot avoid speaking of certain sins which are not only shameful but common.

The present writer has acted as secretary to a committee, which for several years past has endeavoured to answer questions of casuistry submitted to it. In dealing with such questions we have generally consulted the chief Roman Catholic text-books, but we have realised, in nearly every case, that our different circumstances rendered it necessary to form an independent judgment. Believing as we do that the Church in England has rightly returned to the practice of the early Church in not insisting on compulsory confession, and that she rightly aims at helping the penitent to keep his own conscience rather than surrender it into the hands of his priest, we have left open many questions which a more rigorous system would have closed. We have kept in mind an appeal made by the Bishop of Oxford (Dr. Gore) many years ago, on behalf of what he called a new form of casuistry. The old casuistry was largely occupied in discovering the most lenient terms on which a sinner could be restored to the communion of the Church; the new casuistry is the attempt to discover, what is the higher line of conduct suggested by the Christian ideal.

We have not allowed ourselves to forget that the practice of confession has been described as the attempt to obtain spiritual whitewash on the cheapest possible terms. We know that it may, when misused, degenerate into a substitute for genuine repentance, but on the other hand we have abundant evidence that the practice of confession, rightly used, brings untold blessings to both priests and people. It is much to be regretted that none of our official Professors of Pastoral Theology seem disposed to take in hand the task of providing the clergy who are called to this ministry with the guidance that they need. There are excellent hand-books for the clergy on preaching, on parochial work, on the management of schools and charitable relief, and some of great value on the priest's inner life, but therc is scarcely any book which one can recommend as a satisfactory and sufficient manual for a young priest, when he finds himself drawing near to the time when he will have the responsibility of hearing confessions. It is said that a young priest asked the late Bishop of Lincoln (Dr. King) what he could read to fit himself for this ministry, and the Bishop, whose experience as a guide of souls was almost unrivalled in the Anglican communion, replied, "Read the Bible and good novels." The writer cannot vouch for the accuracy of the story, but the reply was eminently characteristic. The reading of good novels tends to increase one's knowledge of human nature, and to cultivate what may be called the instincts of a gentleman, and a priest who knows and loves his Bible is so far equipped for the "ministry of the Word," but the words of the Bishop should not be quoted to excuse the neglect of technical knowledge. The individual cannot safely ignore the accumulated experience of others who have exercised this ministry, or disregard rules which have the stamp of catholic authority.

Without possessing the ability or the leisure to attempt a formal treatise on this great subject, I venture to offer to the younger clergy some counsels which one has derived in part from the study of Anglican and Roman authorities, in part from the experience gained in missions or in ordinary parochial work, and above all from conference with others who have largely used the ministry of absolution. To those who are called to the office and work of priests in the Church of God, and who desire to make full proof of their ministry, I venture to commend some words taken from Dr. Pusey's famous sermon on the Entire Absolution of the Penitent.

"Blessed as this office is, and like our Blessed Lord's

own to relieve the burden of the clogged and choked heart by receiving it, still from the experience of those who have exercised that holy ministry, it must be said that there is none so full of peril to those who have not, by penitence and mortification, and the continual sanctifying grace of God, or by some sharp, penetrating, severing stroke, been deadened to the things of time, and in the full aim and desire of their heart are seeking to live to God. Sin is an awful thing to handle. To hear of it continually and not be defiled with it nor dulled to it; to compassionate a fellow-sinner and be austere with self; to hear of the defilement of every sense and keep watch over his own, comes not from man himself, but from the continual persevering and refreshing grace of God, which keeps the whole man stayed upon, looking to, and sealed by Him. It is, then, a call the more to us to cleave fast to God, that those committed to our charge may rightly place trust in us; to be jealously watchful over ourselves, guard speech habitually, if we are to receive the solemn secrets of men's inmost souls: train ourselves in holy discipline, that we may be fitted to train others, not be blind leaders of the blind; strict with ourselves, that we may know how to be tenderly careful of others; hate all motions of sin in ourselves that we may teach others to hate it with a holy shrinking; be fervent ourselves that we may inspire others with a holy fervour; love Him much who we trust hath forgiven us, that we may teach others, being much forgiven, much to love; and study deep humility, and fervent prayer lest we fall into the snare of the devil. For as the reward is great so is the peril."

II

CONFESSION AND LIBERTY

It cannot be necessary to occupy much time or space here in demonstrating that the Church of England, in common with the whole Catholic Church East and West, teaches that our Lord Jesus Christ left to His Church authority and power to carry on His work in the absolution, or remission, of sins.

Whatever different shades there may be in the private opinions of the Bishops of the Anglican communion, every one of them in the execution of his office says to those whom he ordains:—

"Receive the Holy Ghost for the office and work of a priest in the Church of God, now committed unto thee by the imposition of our hands. Whose sins thou dost forgive they are forgiven; and whose sins thou dost retain they are retained."

Behind the words of the Prayer-book lie those of the Gospel, and those who believe that our Lord Jesus Christ rose from the dead, have no reason to doubt that on the first Easter night He said to His apostles, "Peace be unto you; as My Father hath sent Me even so I send you," with the words already quoted from the ordinal. It is of little consequence whether the words were addressed to representatives of the whole Church (S. Luke tells us that others were with the eleven), or to the Apostles alone, as S. John seems to suggest. It is not contended that the great commission was given to the Apostles, as isolated or independent of the Body, and if it were given to the Body as a whole, it is a charge which must be executed through the organs of the Body. It is clear that the Church of England is committed to the belief that the right to exercise in the Church's name this power of absolution is entrusted to the priesthood. Whether there are, or ought to be, any restrictions on its use is a point for further consideration, but *prima facie*, and in the absence of any regulation to the contrary, every priest may be called upon by those, whose souls are entrusted to his care, to hear confessions and absolve both sick and whole.

It is more to our present purpose to observe how far the Church of England differs from the Church of Rome, in the use she proposes to make of the power which she claims to possess.

Dr. Pusey observes, "The point at issue between the Romanists and ourselves as to confession relates (as they themselves admit) not to its general advantage, or its necessity in particular cases, or its use as a means of discipline, or to the desirableness of public confession before the whole Church, or the great difficulty of true penitence without it, or the duty of individuals to comply with it if the Church requires it; but it is whether confession to man be so essential to absolution that the benefits of absolution cannot be had without it."

I am quoting from Note M in the translation of Tertullian, *de Penitentia,* from the *Oxford Library of the Fathers,* and there Dr. Pusey examines at considerable length the patristic passages, which are alleged in support of the famous decree of the Lateran Council.

It was in 1215 that it was laid down "that every faithful Christian of either sex after he has come to years of discretion shall once in the year at least confess his own sins to his own priest; and shall strive with all his strength to fulfil the penance laid upon him, reverently receiving the sacrament of the Eucharist at least at Easter . . . otherwise in life he shall be debarred from entering the Church and in death he shall lack Christian burial."

Here is the law which binds the conscience of all who are subject to the Roman obedience, and the Council of Trent anathematises "any who say that in the sacrament of penance it is not of Divine right, necessary to the remission of sins, to confess all and each mortal sin, whereof memory is had, after previous, due, and diligent thought, including secret sins, and such as are against the two last commands of the decalogue, and the circumstances which change the character of the sin."

It is not difficult to show that this is a doctrine which goes a very long way beyond the teaching of the Fathers, who are quoted in its support. The theological student will find in Dr. Pusey's elaborate note the principal passages on which the controversy in this respect between Rome and Canterbury turns, and whoso has time and patience may read in the learned, if prejudiced, pages of Dr. Lea a melancholy history of the attempts to enforce compulsory confession, and of the moral evils which were in his opinion the natural and inevitable result.

The general conclusion that Dr. Pusey reaches after an exhaustive study of the Fathers is "that the early Church had no obligatory confession except that of overt acts of sin with a view to public penitence, and consequently that confession as now practised in the Roman Church is not essential to the validity of the general exercise of the power of the keys; still as a matter of discipline it belongs to the Christian prudence of any Church to imitate it or to lay it aside."

There is in many minds a confusion between the public penance, which ought to be exercised in the case of open and notorious sinners, and the private ministry to individuals, who are drawn by their own conscience alone to desire the benefit of absolution.

The Church of England is deeply committed to the statement that it is much to be wished that the ancient discipline should be restored. Year after year we are reminded in the Commination Service "that in the Primitive Church there was a godly discipline that at the beginning of Lent such persons as stood convicted of notorious sin were put to open penance."

The lack of public discipline is indeed a grievous scandal, and nothing is so likely to shake the allegiance of her children to the Church of England as the admission of persons to Holy Communion who are known to be living in wilful sin, or in flagrant disobedience to the Church's law. The general disregard of obligation to the rules of the Church is largely due to the fact that children have been baptized without any attempt to secure that they shall be brought up in the knowledge and obedience of the Christian law. When the fences have been thrown down at the threshold of the Christian life, it is not surprising that our wisest teachers lament as the gravest evil of the Church the prevalence of membership without any sense of obligation.

Our present concern is with the administration of private and voluntary penance, but in Chapter XI.

will be found some account of its relation to primitive discipline.

We cannot enforce confession, and I hope that we have no wish to do so. The Church of England is well within her rights in holding that the famous decree of the Lateran Council is not binding on her children. Recent controversies have done much to clear the air, and the conference at Fulham in 1902 shows that there is a large measure of agreement between the best representatives of various schools of thought. The volume on confession and absolution by Dr. Drury, now Bishop of Ripon, published in the following year, shows how a learned and devout Evangelical can appreciate the Catholic position, when it is stated by such a careful and exact theologian as Dr. Robert Moberly (see pages 106, 209).

We may take as the deliberate expression of the mind of the Church of England, the following passage from the Charge of Archbishop Temple in 1898:—

"The Church of England, in this as in so many other matters, makes for freedom.

"In the first place the Church insists that the resort to confession shall be altogether and always voluntary. No compulsion, direct or indirect, is ever allowed. No priest has a right to require confession as a condition of being presented for Confirmation, or being admitted to Holy Communion. To claim such a power is a usurpation to be resisted in every way. If any one wishes to confess, the permission to do so is acknowledged in the Prayer-book, and if the need of it be strongly felt, not only acknowledged but encouraged. Every man who comes to Holy Communion is required to be at peace with his own conscience, and if he be perplexed, and cannot find the peace which is required, he is encouraged to come to God's minister for advice. Sometimes a man who has wronged his neighbour does not see how he is to set the wrong right. Sometimes a man who has been fighting with a besetting sin, and fighting unsuccessfully, wants advice in the conduct of his battle. Sometimes a man is troubled with an uneasy feeling that all is not right with him, but he hardly knows in what the worry consists. In such cases as these the man is encouraged to come to God's minister to be told what to do, and if he needs it to be assured as far as man can assure him that God forgives his sin. This assurance is like the decision of an inferior Court—it may be overruled in the Court above, but nevertheless it is of value as far as it goes, and the man may trust it, and act upon it for the present emergency. The same general rule applies to the case of a man in serious sickness. He is to be exhorted, if he feels his conscience troubled with any weighty matter, to make special confession of his sins, and absolution is ordered to be pronounced if he shall heartily and humbly desire it. In this case, as in the other, the confession is made to depend on the conscience being troubled. The initiative is with the man himself; he is to confess if he is troubled, and to seek absolution if he feels the need of it. It is obvious that a confession voluntarily made under pressure of perplexity and trouble is a very different thing from confession as a regular custom enforced with heavy sanctions."

Perhaps some of my readers hold, that the Archbishop's utterance was intended to allay the protestant agitation, which was then at its height, and is only another instance of the spirit of compromise, which makes for weakness and inefficiency. I am afraid it must be confessed that many are glad to accept the Archbishop's defence of confession so far as it goes, but make little or no effort to use the ministry of absolution under the conditions which he lays down; while in fact some of those who are most diligent and effective in bringing souls to repentance look elsewhere for guidance.

So far as the Archbishop himself was concerned the reproach is unfounded. He was certainly not wanting in the courage of his convictions; he heard many confessions himself, and was profoundly convinced of the value of that ministry. It is said that he once surprised his candidates for ordination by saying, "Before long you will have to hear confessions. I suppose you say you are not fit. That is quite true, but you have got to get fit." It is then in entire loyalty to the voluntary system of the Church of England that we desire to become better qualified for our ministry in this respect, and we find that we cannot get the help we need from Roman Catholic sources. The adaptation of foreign manuals to the supposed needs of the English Churchman is never a very satisfactory business. If the editor is nervously anxious to eliminate all that might give offence, he will probably omit much of real value, and in any case his work will retain an exotic flavour, which will not commend it to those who believe that the English Church has a moral standard and a genius of her own. Now, apart from the precept of the Roman Church that confession is binding on all Christians once a year at least, it is admitted that confession is not required from those who are free from deadly sin; and we have good reason to believe that many Christians are in that happy state.

In the *Life of Cardinal Manning*[1] we find a striking and unexpected testimony to the blameless and beautiful lives lived by many in the English Church. He is blaming his co-religionists for their failure to recognise "that the greater part of the

[1] Purcell's *Life*, vol. ii. p. 780.

English people are baptized and therefore are in the supernatural state of grace."

He denies the propositions (1) that they have lost their baptismal grace by mortal sin, and (2) that therefore as they have not the sacrament of Penance they have no means of rising again to the grace of Baptism.

He says, "I have intimately known souls, living by faith, hope, and charity and the sanctifying grace with the seven gifts of the Holy Ghost, in humility, absolute purity of life and heart, in constant meditation on Holy Scripture, unceasing prayer, complete self-denial, personal work amongst the poor; in a word, living lives of visible sanctification. as undoubtedly the work of the Holy Ghost as I have ever seen. I have seen this in whole families, rich and poor, and in all conditions of life. Moreover, I have received into the Church I do not know how many souls in whom I could find no mortal sin."

One cannot refrain from asking in passing the obvious question—Why not let well alone? If the Church of England can tram such saints, why should they be received into another communion? But I only quote these words to establish the point that, in the judgment of this experienced confessor, there are many of the children of the Church of England, who preserve their baptismal innocence and are free from deadly sin.

The frank recognition of this fact will make us quite content not to insist on sacramental confession as being necessary for all; and we shall be much more anxious to bring sinners to repentance than to impose a burden on scrupulous consciences. It is not a satisfactory state of things that, in some parishes where confession is clearly taught, it is used by the inner circle of devout souls, who might make very good progress in holiness without it, while it is neglected by the sort of people who need it very badly, because, as it may be they themselves know, without it they cannot return to a state of grace, or approach at all to the Table of the Lord. We should be in a much healthier state, and one much more resembling the conditions of the primitive Church, if the use of confession were much more common amongst the new converts, or in the main body of sorely-tempted communicants; while the devout souls, presumably free from deadly sin, made less demands upon the attention of the clergy.

The late Bishop of Salisbury (Dr. Wordsworth), in a letter on the ministry of penitence addressed to the clergy of his diocese in 1898, has some excellent remarks on the kind of people who need confession; "I think that there are many persons living with heavy sin upon their consciences, sin perhaps that has found expression in single, dark acts, or sin that has become habitual, who would be very much helped by confession. To such it may make all the difference between interior light and darkness. Such confession may need to be repeated, perhaps at regular intervals, in order to test the progress and perseverance of the penitent. There are others of scrupulous conscience, who may be made easy and at peace by it, who should, nevertheless, in their own interest not be advised to seek it often. There are many others to whom I would say, as S. Jerome does to Demetrias (Ep. 130, 9), 'Nos ignoremus poenitentiam ne facile peccemus. Illa quasi secunda post naufragium miseris tabula sit; in virgine integra servetur navis.' A Christian virgin should not need that second plank of penitence; it is meant for those who have made shipwreck of life, that by it they may escape safe to land."

III

CHRISTIAN HOLINESS

It must be clear to any candid reader of the previous chapters that the writer has no desire to press the practice of confession beyond the limits laid down in the Book of Common Prayer, as they are defined by representative Anglican authorities such as Andrewes, Hooker, and Pusey, or to come down to our day, by the late Archbishop of Canterbury and Bishop Wordsworth of Salisbury.

Moreover, he does not assume that the graver sins which chiefly need confession are so common, that the priest should treat the souls committed to his care as though they were in need of continual restoration to a state of grace, from which they were continually falling away.

Where infant baptism is practised under right conditions, we hope that many persons make orderly progress, going on from strength to strength. The christened child, taught to pray in his earliest infancy, growing up in the atmosphere of faith and love, and responding to genuine Christian education, gradually develops a character which is marked by personal devotion to our Lord and growing conformity to His Will. From early years he learns that religious faith and moral conduct are for the child of God inseparable.

He knows that he cannot please God except by doing His Will, and that His Will includes not only the duties which are primarily religious, but the duties also which he owes to his neighbours and himself. The wide range of these duties is only gradually perceived, and it is the main duty of the Christian teacher to stimulate and encourage the highest aspiration.

Nothing is so deadening to the spiritual life as the notion that the chief business of the clergy is to keep men free from gross sins, and to restore them when they have fallen, in order to secure the observance of a conventional standard. We are more concerned, as Christians, with the Beatitudes than with the Ten Commandments, and the fruits of the Spirit make better heads for self-examination than the seven deadly sins. The ordinary Christian, and not merely the exceptional saint, is called to the imitation of Christ, because He "suffered for us, leaving us an example that we should follow in His steps" (1 Pet. ii. 21).

And yet it is impossible to ignore the fact of sin. Just in proportion to the earnestness with which a man tries to respond to this call he is conscious of failure, and he knows that failure is due not only to temptation from without, but to an inherent weakness in himself. Now, this inherent weakness is what we call original sin, and the recognition of its reality and power is the first condition of moral and spiritual growth. Robert Browning saw one of the strongest reasons for believing the truth of the Christian faith in this:—

> "'Tis the faith that launched point-blank her dart
> At the head of a lie—taught original sin,
> The corruption of man's heart."
>
> *Gold Hair: a Story of Pornic.*

We are not now concerned with the ultimate explanation of original sin. The narrative of the fall in Genesis iii. may be regarded as an allegory, and it does not answer our questions as to the ultimate origin of evil, but it does correspond, in a very striking way, with the teaching of biology, and with facts of experience only too familiar.

Biologists tell us how the embryo child in its mother's womb passes through stages which reflect and reproduce the characteristics of its animal ancestry; we know too well that we may find in ourselves the ferocity of a tiger, the cold-blooded selfishness of the fish, and the greediness, not to say the uncleanness, of the pig. This corruption of the heart, which we find universal, confirms the inspired allegory, which teaches us that something went wrong at the beginning of human history. Man was scarcely conscious of the spiritual life, which distinguished him from the animal world to which he was akin, before he exercised his new capacity for choice in the wrong way, and chose the path of disobedience and self-indulgence, bringing upon the race its heritage of guilt and woe. However we explain it, the fact remains, and to borrow the words of Archbishop Temple—

"We mean to say that sin is not something which has penetrated into our nature from the outside; that it is not a garment thrown over our shoulders, which may therefore be slipped off like a garment; that it is not the result of evil example, or of any external influence whatever; that it is not learnt like a lesson of evil, nor caught like an infectious disease. It is part of our very selves. It has its springs in the very sources of our being. It mingles its poison with the very first beginnings of our life, whether spiritual or natural. It cannot be cast off. It cannot be torn up by the roots. It cannot be treated by any medicine which discipline, or education, or example can supply. Penetrate into man as deeply as you will, and you cannot reach its origin; drill him almost into a machine, and you will not kill the life of this fatal power. Nay, it sometimes seems as if by long drilling you might kill everything else; kill affection and stifle impulse, and dry up the imagination, and convert the reason itself into a mere engine for producing arguments at need; and yet you will not kill the inborn spirit of evil; some day by some accident it is roused to unusual violence, and bursts through all fetters, and reasserts its independence as the last, and in this world imperishable, token of humanity" (*Rugby Sermons*).

It is because sin is so deeply rooted in the human heart that the pursuit of holiness and the deepening of penitence are really inseparable. Even the saints who through God's mercy have been preserved from overt sin like David's, find it natural to say, "Behold, I was shapen in wickedness, and in sin hath my mother conceived me. But lo! Thou requirest truth in the inward parts, and shall make me to understand wisdom secretly." As the ninth article rightly insists, "This infection of nature doth remain, yea in them that are regenerated."

There is, however, an immense difference between the condition of those who preserve their baptismal innocence, growing in grace and producing the fruits of the Spirit, and those who by wilful and deliberate sin fall away, so something must be said about the distinction between venial and deadly sin.

The value of the distinction is often questioned. Dr. Moberly said at the Fulham Conference, "This distinction is true and valuable, if not pressed. The older distinction was with *levia*, *gravia*, and *gravissima*, which are obviously indefinite words. But the moment words of degree are pressed into technical distinctions of kind, the definition which aimed at truth has passed into untruth."

The distinction is clearly marked in the 1st Epistle of St. John. In 1 St. John v. 16, we read, "There is a sin unto death," and in the next verse, "All unrighteousness is sin; and there is a sin not unto death." With this may be compared the earlier statements: iii. 6, "Whoso abideth in Him sinneth not," and i. 10, "If we say that we have no sin, we make Him a liar, and His word is not in us." From these words we infer that St. John means that the normal condition of a Christian abiding in Christ is one of freedom from deadly sin, but not of freedom from all sin; and this distinction between sins great and small is recognised by men in general, though difficulties arise when an attempt is made to introduce a rigid classification.

The gravity of sin depends not on the sin itself so much as on the state of the person who commits it, and it is very dangerous to suggest that any sin is insignificant. The broad fact that certain sins are deadly, in that they tend to cut off the soul from God, can scarcely be denied; against such we are taught to pray in the Litany, where we ask to be delivered from fornication and all other deadly sin. There, a certain sin, not reckoned as a crime to be punished by human law, is regarded as deadly in itself and typical of others like it. Where souls are awakened to the call of God, and to the supreme obligation of holiness, there will be a real anxiety to know whether they have transgressed the line between what is merely venial and what carries with it the appalling consequence of separation from God. The troubled conscience can be best guided not so much by technical rules, as by the experience of a priest, penitent himself, who can enter into anxieties which he himself has felt. He will know how to make allowance for a soul struggling bravely with temptations, which are partly the consequence of past and forgiven sin; he will encourage the weak in their effort after holiness; he will warn the self-satisfied against the danger of indifference to little sins. But, above all, the true priest is not content to absolve the penitents who fall short of some conventional standard. He is concerned with their progressive growth in holiness, "admonishing every man and teaching every man in all wisdom, that we may present every man perfect in Christ."

The hearing of confessions and the ministry of absolution is only one department of what S. Gregory calls "Ars artium regimen animarum," but since sin is the chronic disease affecting the whole human race, one cannot promote genuine growth in holiness without the discovery of sin.

The business of the spiritual physician is to keep in vigorous health the souls committed to his care, but he cannot do it without some systematic study of the manifold ramifications of the disease to which all are liable, and the remedies appropriate to each.

In S. Chrysostom's treatise on the priesthood, a striking parallel is drawn between the position of the spiritual and the natural shepherd. The natural shepherd, when he perceives that one of his sheep is sick, can get hold of it and apply the proper remedy. He can tie it up and diminish its food, or apply cautery or the knife; but with the spiritual shepherd it is not so, for in his case the taking of the remedy depends not on the will of the shepherd, but on the will of his sheep (*De Sacerdotio*, ii. 3).

Pastoral work worthy of the name involves a personal relation between the pastor and his flock; and clergy misconceive the function of their office if they regard themselves merely as lecturers on religion, or organisers of public worship; and even these functions are sometimes neglected for much less important forms of clerical activity. It is, indeed, a lamentable fact that the energies of the clergy are sometimes absorbed in work which, however excellent in itself, is utterly remote from prayer and the ministry of the Word.

The ministry of the Word includes not only public preaching and the instruction of classes, but the application of the Word of God to individual souls. Without some recognised mode of pastoral intercourse this is impossible. Some would say that the system of house-to-house visitation, which is probably pursued with greater diligence by the clergy of the Church of England than by any other religious teachers in the world, supplies all that is needed. I should be very sorry to disparage that important part of ministerial work, but it is absurd to say that pastoral visitation covers the ground or supplies all that is needed. Those who have the deepest sense of pastoral responsibility are the first to acknowledge how much of their time is wasted in the kind of pastoral calls which degenerate into merely social visits, or are merely the occasions of distributing charitable relief. In the afternoon, when the diligent curate habitually goes on his rounds, he generally finds only the women at home, and they, busy at the household duties, are not always ready to receive the ministry of the Word or to join in prayer. The curate who is thoughtful as well as diligent visits in the evening, when the men are at home, and that is better, but it does not necessarily secure that he gets the man to himself, and can speak to him of personal religion. Sometimes he has a better chance if he joins the ploughman at his work, and walks beside him while he ploughs his lonely furrow. The priest with a real pastoral instinct will find his opportunity as best he can, but there is no hope of making pastoral intercourse a reality for all who need it, till people learn that they will find the parish priest in his church at stated times, at regular and frequent intervals, prepared to guide his people one by one along the way of holiness whether they need confession or no

The physician of the body does not do his work by giving public lectures on health and disease, or by suggesting that every sufferer may choose for himself an appropriate pill or potion: even so the spiritual physician can neither cure the disease of sin, nor promote spiritual health and vigour, unless his flock will come and tell him what is the matter, or let him see how God is leading them on from strength to strength.

It is here that we touch the important point of spiritual direction, which is quite distinct from confession. There is a real danger of confusion. Many a penitent who needs from time to time the benefit of absolution needs no other director than the Holy Spirit. The priest must not assume dominion over souls. His business is not to relieve the penitent of his own responsibility, or to regulate for him the details of his conduct. He must rather strive to bring him into such a relation to the Holy Spirit that the enlightened conscience needs little or no human guidance.

A lady of my acquaintance told me that she had once asked a priest for advice, and he said that he would be happy to give it, if she would place herself under his direction. She naturally asked what that involved, and he replied that she must be prepared to surrender into his keeping her conscience, her reason, and her will! I hope the lady misunderstood him, for, of course such a monstrous claim would not be made by any instructed priest in the Anglican communion, but it cannot be too clearly said, that direction should involve nothing of the sort. Wise direction aims not at the enslaving of the conscience or the stifling of the reason, but at its liberty and enlightenment, and the best confessors are they whose penitents quickly learn to be strong and free, and as little as possible dependent on priestly help. And yet, at any rate in the earlier stages of conversion, there is much for the priest to do in suggesting a rule of life and methods of prayer. Many Christians fail to advance in holiness, not so much for lack of good intentions, as because they have not learned to adjust means to ends, and to map out for themselves a course of conduct. If they are willing to learn, an experienced confessor can be of great service. With tact and sympathy he can bring the experience he has gained to bear upon the circumstances of each individual, and suggest, though he refuses to dictate, the plans which are most likely to promote a real advance. Here is the true casuistry, which does not concern itself so much with sin, as with the discovery of the highest attainable standard of holiness. Some suggestions about the counsels that may be given will be found in Chapter X.

IV

THE PASTORAL OFFICE

GRANTING that confession in the presence of a priest has a legitimate place in the system of the Church of England, it is worth while to inquire why it is so little used, especially by those who need it most. The blame must surely rest mainly with the clergy. Too often our ministry is so vague and ineffectual that it does not reach the conscience and induce any real anxiety about sin; and when the conscience is not really stirred, people will readily accept the teaching of those who cry "Peace, peace, where there is no peace." And the clergy who really desire to be more thorough are exposed to a steady pressure exerted in favour of so-called moderation. A priest who is resolved "constantly to speak the truth and boldly rebuke vice" must be prepared to "suffer for the truth's sake." The practice of confession is unpopular, and the very mention of it may disturb the peace of a parish. The influential laity, whose financial support of the Church is held to be of immense importance, and sometimes even the Bishops, bring a steady pressure to bear upon a priest. They expect him to be complacent and popular, and, above all, to avoid anything which is likely to give offence.

For a while these easygoing ways appear to serve their purpose, but sooner or later the clergy who acquiesce in the suppression of troublesome questions find themselves without any influence for good. They are regarded by their flocks with indifference, if not with contempt: as a spiritual force they do not count. They may gain, at any rate for a time, rewards which the world bestows on those who serve it well, but they know nothing of the deeper joys of the ministry—the undying gratitude of souls saved from sin and brought home to GOD, the consciousness of fellowship with Christ, and with His saints.

I do not mean that we are bound to preach confession in season and out of season; still less that we are to transgress the limits of Anglican orthodoxy by insisting on its necessity in every case. To do so would be wrong, foolish, and useless. Wrong, because it is not according to the mind of the Church which we serve, foolish and useless because it will repel, rather than attract, the people who need confession most. There is only one way. The priest who would teach confession must be a penitent himself. How can he expound the system of the Church, in a way which will reach the hearts of the people, if he has never felt the shame and sorrow of confession, or the joy of absolution?

But it may be urged that, even on the Roman principle mentioned in Chapter II., confession is not needed for those who are free from deadly sin. For the sake of argument let us suppose that priests have no personal experience of deadly sin. It is a large assumption, and perhaps it ignores the fact that what is merely venial in one person may be deadly in another. The priest, who may have been preserved throughout his life from any approach to the grosser forms of intemperance or lust, can scarcely claim that he has never been touched by pride or anger, avarice and sloth, and the guilt of such sins must be measured by the height of his calling and the width of his responsibility.

But, if the sins of a priest are clearly venial, if he never has reason to doubt the reality of his own forgiveness, and the security of his own union with God, he has to deal with some at least who are fallen. His ministry is not confined to those who are as innocent and happy as himself; he must know what to say to those who are grieved and wearied with the burden of their sin. He will surely do so best if he has put himself into the position of the man who cries, "God be merciful to me a sinner."

In the absence of anything like deadly sin, one

may well use confession as a means of discipline, as an exercise in humility, as a way of bringing oneself up from time to time to the judgment of the Church.

When the consciences of the faithful laity are stirred they look round for some one to whom they can unburden themselves; and it is, indeed, a grievous reproach to a diocese if it numbers amongst its clergy few, if any, to whom the penitent feel that they can turn for sympathy and help.

The unreadiness of the English clergy to minister to troubled consciences is illustrated by a scene in one of George Eliot's greatest novels. In *Adam Bede* the Rev. Arthur Irwine is typical of the sort of English clergyman who is thoroughly approved by those who ask for moderation. He was quite free from "enthusiasm," and equally opposed to Methodism and Popery. When the young squire, Arthur Donnithorne, was on the brink of deadly sin, he rode over one morning to have breakfast with the rector, for whom he entertained sincere respect and affection. The rector was quite prepared to moralise and give excellent advice on general principles, and indeed suspected that the young man had something on his mind, but serious confessions are not made at the breakfast table, and to clergymen who are not prepared to say that they have been entrusted with the power of absolution.

The opportunity was lost, and the young man, hovering on the brink of deadly and irreparable sin, found no restraint in the vague generalities of his clerical friend. We know the sequel; but the tragedy of Hetty Sorrel is typical of innumerable others, which are as common as they are, largely because we lack a watchful and an effective ministry of the Gospel.

How different might have been the story had this amiable clergyman taught his pupil that there is an effectual remedy for sin and a real preservative against it. There was the young man ready to open his heart; with a little sympathy he might have been induced to make a real confession. At that stage he might so easily have been set free, and his absolution would, of course, have depended on the readiness to break off the foolish intercourse which, unchecked, led to the ruin of the girl and the subsequent murder of her child.

On the other hand, the practice of confession is rendered repulsive, not to evil livers, but to serious and conscientious people, because it has sometimes been associated with moral laxity. One who reads Pascal's *Provincial Letters* cannot be surprised that the casuistry of the Jesuits, which he has exposed with such merciless severity, provoked a terrible reaction. Their desperate efforts to reconcile the practice of religion with the manners and customs of the world have not only compromised the reputation of the "Society of Jesus," they have rendered the legitimate and wholesome use of confession far more difficult.

The foundation of a better system must be laid in the conversion of the priesthood. It is only men who are penitent themselves who can hope to hear the confessions of their people, when confession is established on a voluntary basis. There is abundant evidence that men and women in the Church of England are ready enough to use confession, when they can find priests who are worthy of their confidence. Looking back over the past sixty years one can think of a goodly company of men who were trusted guides, not because they had conspicuous talents for preaching or organisation, but because they were known to be lovers of souls, who believed in the exercise of their priesthood. Now that they have passed away all men honour Dr. Pusey and Bishop King, G. H. Wilkinson and George Body. Those good men would all have said that the best work they did for our Lord and His Church was not in public but in the private ministry to individual souls. If this is so, surely the time has come to recognise more fully that our clergy should be ready and better prepared for the exercise of their ministry; and the preparation must be twofold: first there must be the deepening of our own spiritual life, and secondly there must be the acquisition of a certain amount of technical knowledge.

The former is of much greater importance than the latter, and it is far less easily acquired. There is no infallible system for producing it, but to go into retreat for three or four days of continuous spiritual exercises, under the guidance of some experienced confessor, often makes all the difference to a priest's conception of the meaning and responsibility of his work.

So called quiet days are a very poor substitute for a real retreat, and are chiefly valuable as the opportunity of suggesting that something more is needed. They are almost purely mischievous if they leave us under the impression that our present standards of spiritual life, and pastoral work, are satisfactory.

It is in a long retreat, when one gives up three or four days to the solemn consideration of fundamental questions, and is led through the successive stages of the purgative, the illuminative, and the unitive way, that the priest is really humbled before God, and goes back to take up his ministry in a more serious fashion.

Retreats have been fairly common in the Church of England for forty years, and they are valued increasingly by a considerable number of devout lay folk, but a very small proportion of the clergy seem to use them, and the result is that many of the laity, who really care for deeper spiritual things, do not know where to turn for the comfort, and the counsel, and the gift of absolution which they have the right to expect.

It may be said that the ministry of absolution is so difficult and delicate a matter that its exercise should be confined to priests specially qualified and licensed for the purpose. A largely-signed petition was addressed to Convocation in 1873 desiring that the Bishops should appoint a body of licensed confessors to whom this ministry might be confined, and this demand seemed not unreasonable.

It was then rejected, for the great majority of the Bishops would do nothing to encourage the practice of confession, and public opinion in the Church was not ripe for such a clear assertion of its legitimate place.

It is still held by many thoughtful people that the Bishops should regulate the practice, and it is thought to be little short of a scandal, that a young priest of twenty-four may be speedily immersed in the practice of hearing the confessions of both sexes. In answer to this it may be observed that such cases are very rare. In those parishes where the use of confession is general, the vicar may be trusted to regulate the matter. He, and his experienced assistants, will hear the confessions of men and women and girls, while the young priest within two or three years of his ordination, if he hears confessions at all, will only hear those of young men and boys, whose confidence he can win more easily than it could be won by an older man. Moreover, where confession is voluntary and people are entirely free to choose their own confessor, they are not likely to go to those who are wholly unfit. There is a simple rule which one generally gives to those who ask where they should go—"Do not make your confession to one who does not go to confession himself." People soon find out, by his preaching and general way of life, whether a priest is likely to be of use to them or not. Moreover, the hearing of confessions cannot be separated from the general exercise of the ministry. A priest at his ordination receives his commission, and when he is licensed by the Bishop to a cure of souls, he is sent with his Prayer-book in his hand to visit the sick and dying. If he is a faithful minister of repentance the sick and dying will sometimes desire to open their grief, even when he is not obliged by the Prayer-book to urge them to do so. Sometimes, no doubt, the young priest may be able to procure for the sick and dying an experienced confessor, but in many cases he must trust in GOD and do his best, for, in the absence of any restriction, his cure of souls impels him to exercise the commission which he has received.

Again, if it were seriously proposed to provide in each diocese a certain number of licensed confessors, it is certain that the priests best fitted for this difficult and delicate office would shrink very much from assuming a peculiar position, which marked them off from their brother clergy. The faithful laity can be trusted to find out the best confessors for themselves, and they would not be grateful for the appointment of diocesan officials, whose qualifications had not been gained in the school of experience.

On the other hand, much is to be said in favour of reserved cases. In the absence of any regulation the Anglican theory appears to be, that any licensed priest may absolve any penitent after any sin, however great.

The general commission to "remit and retain" bestowed in ordination is, of course, limited by the Bishop's licence. A priest without a Bishop's licence has no jurisdiction. In the Roman Church he would not think of celebrating the Eucharist or hearing confessions without "faculties" With us much greater laxity is common, but loyal and conscientious priests do not feel justified in exercising their ministry except in the sphere assigned to them.

It is no doubt quite legitimate for a priest licensed in one diocese to officiate in another for a limited period, if the diocesan custom permits it, but he is subject at any moment to the Bishop's inhibition, and he cannot officiate in the church or parish of another priest without his permission. It is very desirable that the clergy who hear confessions should be careful to observe this canonical obligation; and there is urgent need of some further regulation on the part of the Bishops.

In comparing our theory and practice with that of the Roman Catholic Church we notice, that in that communion certain cases fall under the ordinary jurisdiction of the parish priest, while others are reserved to the Bishop, and others are reserved to the Pope. Indeed, the modern Roman theory appears to be that the Pope is the sole fountain of justice and mercy, and Bishops and priests are only his delegates. With us, of course, the Bishop is the disciplinary authority for his own diocese—bound, however, by the canons of his own province and of the Church Universal; and it would seem right for him to determine how much of his authority he delegates to the parish priests, whom he institutes, and to other priests whom he licenses.

Would it not be well if the Bishop were to avail himself of the experience of the Roman Church and reserve certain cases? In the Roman obedience the cases reserved differ in various dioceses, and in missionary jurisdictions (such as England was in their estimation till two or three years ago) the largest powers are entrusted to the priests on the mission.

The point of most practical importance in which the present writer earnestly desires that the Bishops would take action has to do with the confessions of priests. Supposing a priest falls into sin so grave that in the eyes of all Christian people, if the facts were known, he would seem unfit to exercise his ministry, until after some long period of penance, it is bad that he should be able to quiet his conscience and celebrate at once, by making his confession and receiving absolution from a priest of his own selection, who may lack the knowledge, the experience, and the courage to deal with such a case. It would be far better if the clergy generally were instructed, that their faculties and licence to pronounce absolution were subject to some limitation. Certain cases might be reserved to the Bishop himself, or to a priest appointed by him with special authority to deal with cases of a very grave character. If the principle of reserved cases were once established it would give the opportunity to raise the moral standard, and prevent the growing laxity, which is encouraged by careless or ignorant confessors, who may pass lightly over certain offences, which ought to be condemned and severely punished. By way of illustration take the case of a certain grave sin. To its honour be it said, the Roman Catholic Church consistently condemns certain practices in married life, which are contrary to God's law, and injurious to the race, and the clergy refuse to absolve those who will not promise amendment. Amongst ourselves some clergy take the stricter line, but if they are not supported by the Bishops and their brethren, even well-disposed people may come to think lightly of the sin. The present writer is not suggesting that inquiry must be made into secret sins. People are quite free to avoid confession, and communicate, if they can on their own responsibility; but if they ask for absolution they should be told plainly that they cannot be absolved, unless they promise to abandon practices, which the Church refuses to tolerate.

V

THE LATIN RULES

In the *Priest's 'Book of Private Devotion*, an excellent manual widely used by the English clergy, the editors have printed in the original rules taken from the Roman *Rituale* which, they justly remark, sum up in brief compass all that is most necessary for confessors to know and observe.

I venture to offer a translation with some brief notes.

I

In order that the holy Sacrament of Penance, instituted by Christ our Lord for the restoration to the grace of God of those who have fallen after baptism, may be duly administered; in the first place let the confessor remember that he plays the part alike of a judge and a physician, and so in order that he may be able to judge rightly between leprosy and leprosy, and like a skilled physician prudently cure the diseases of the soul, and know how to apply to each the appropriate remedies, let him strive to acquire as much science and prudence as he can for that purpose, both by constant prayer to God and by the study of approved authors.

(*a*) Remembering the stricter definition of a sacrament in the Catechism, some may hesitate to use the term "Sacrament of Penance," but they cannot question that the power of absolution was given by our Lord Himself (S. John xx. 23), though it is not tied to an outward and visible sign.

(*b*) We have, I fear, no list of approved authors, but the confessor will find sufficient guidance in some of the books mentioned in Chapter XII.

II

When called to hear a confession let him show himself ready and easy to approach; and before he comes to hear it, if time allows, he will with pious prayers implore Divine help to discharge his ministry in a right and holy way.

It is not enough to be ready to hear confessions if specially asked to do so. The faithful priest should place himself at the disposal of his penitents, by being in church at stated times to receive them.

III

Let him hear confessions in churches, and not in private houses without reasonable cause, and when that occurs let him take care to hear them in a seemly and open place.

We cannot be too careful to avoid scandal. Some quiet corner in the open Church is greatly to be preferred to the vestry. The practice of confession has been greatly hindered by quite unnecessary secrecy. There is much to be said in favour of confessional boxes, and in the Roman Church they secure for priest and penitent that the confession cannot be interrupted or overheard, and there is no possibility of scandal connected with their use. A slight screen serves the same purpose, but sometimes both priests and penitents prefer that their proceedings should be entirely open, and there is no reason for a hard-and-fast rule if the principle stated above is duly observed.

IV

If the penitent is unknown to the priest, he should inquire into his state; and how long ago he made his last confession, and whether he fulfilled the penance imposed upon him. Moreover, whether he had duly and completely made his former confessions; whether he is well grounded in Christian doctrine; whether he has diligently examined his conscience beforehand as he ought? But these and similar questions are better asked at the end than in the beginning of the confession.

More often than not the priest will find it quite unnecessary to ask these questions, but sometimes they are essential if he is to deal thoroughly with the case.

V

If he finds that the penitent is ignorant of the elements of the Christian faith; if time allows let him briefly instruct him in the articles of faith, and other things necessary to be known in order to be saved, and let him reprove his ignorance and warn him to learn them afterwards with greater diligence.

The direct personal dealing with the soul, which confession involves, reveals the need of much more thorough and systematic instruction than the members of the English Church generally receive. Only an experienced confessor knows how lamentable is the ignorance of fundamental truth even amongst regular church-goers and communicants.

VI

Let him hear the penitent with patience and help him as often as he needs it, but never interrupt unless he need to understand something better. But let him inspire confidence and offer kindly help, so that the penitent may rightly and fully confess all his sins, putting away the foolish shame, by which some are hindered at the instigation of the devil and so dare not confess their sins.

VII

If the penitent has not expressed the number and kind of his sins and the circumstances which are necessary to their explanation, the priest must prudently ask him. And if considering the circumstances of the person he has reasonable grounds for fearing or doubting, whether his confession is complete, let him prudently examine him about the things, which he suspects are being kept back by the penitent, especially about the sins common to his state, above all if he has not made any reference to them at all.

VIII

But let him be careful not to hinder any one by curious or useless questions, especially in the case of young people of either sex, or ask them imprudently about things of which they are ignorant, lest they be scandalised and so learn to sin.

The three last rules are of very special importance. It is impossible to exaggerate the harm which may be done by the asking of wrong or foolish questions. If the priest is a good man, protected in his ministry by a vivid sense of the Divine Presence, he is not likely to say what he ought not, but there is a very real danger of injuring the penitent, by failing to help him to be rid of the whole burden on his mind.

The penitent who is treated in a superficial and perfunctory fashion by a timid or careless priest may rejoice at the moment that he is spared the shame of a painful disclosure, but the absolution does not bring him solid, lasting peace, and he may learn to think very lightly of sins half confessed and easily absolved. It is in the delicate matter of knowing how to probe the conscience, and to get at material facts, that the young priest most needs help. He is bound to probe deep enough to know, for example, in a matter of dishonesty whether the case is one in which restitution is needed, or in a matter of keeping bad company whether the penitent is in danger of relapse; whether he is prepared to break off all occasions of sin; and last, not least, whether the sin is of so grave a character that absolution ought not to be given unless the penitent is willing to submit to the judgment of the Bishop, as suggested in the last chapter.

IX

At length, when the confession has been heard, let him with fatherly love administer rebukes and counsels befitting the gravity and quality of the sins, so far as he sees there is need of them, and he will strive with efficacious words to lead the penitent to sorrow and contrition, and induce him to amend his life, place it on a better footing, and tell him the remedies for sins.

Here again discretion is needed. The spiritual tact, which can be won only by experience and sympathy and the continual dependence on the Holy Spirit, is needed. Some penitents need nothing but the absolution, and well-meant counsels and rebukes may only distract them; but others are reasonably disappointed if the confessor has no words of encouragement or exhortation. Generally these should be very short and pointed; sometimes the confessor must be ready to spend an immense amount of time and trouble in helping the penitent to acquire that real sorrow of heart, and firm purpose of amendment, which are really essential to his pardon.

X

Finally, let him impose some wholesome and fitting satisfaction, such as the spirit of prudence suggests, taking account of the state, condition, sex, age, and even the disposition of the penitents.

Let him see that he does not impose on grave sins the most trifling penances, lest, if haply he connive at them, he is made partaker of other men's sins. Let him keep before his eyes the point that the satisfaction should not be merely with a view to guard the new life and heal the infirmity, but for the punishment of past sins.

Great care must be taken lest the "satisfaction" here mentioned should be confounded with the "full, perfect, and sufficient sacrifice, oblation, and satisfaction" offered by our Lord Himself.

It would be a terrible abuse of the ministry of absolution if any penitent were led to suppose that he could offer satisfaction for his sins in that sense, but the desire to suffer something for the past, as well as to guard against sin in the future, is an accompaniment of genuine penitence, of which the confessor must take account.

XI

Let him take care as far as possible to impose penances, which counteract the sins; as on the covetous almsgiving, on the lustful fastings and other mortifications of the flesh, on the proud the duties of humility, on the slothful devotional exercises. In short, let him prescribe on each, those by which he hopes they may be most effectually restrained from sin; especially the daily exercise of prayer, particularly mental prayer, and sacred reading, and the worthy reception of the sacraments. But for secret sins, however grave, he must never impose an outward penance.

The danger of betraying the nature of the sin by inflicting an appropriate penance is obvious, and every careful priest will guard against it, but on the other hand there are cases when the confessor must urge the penitent to prove his sincerity by acknowledging his sin to those who have a right to know it. It is sometimes the duty of a faithless husband or wife to acknowledge his or her guilt to the injured partner; a priest who has rendered himself unfit for his ministry must sometimes be urged to place himself in the hands of his Bishop; a criminal may be obliged to give himself up to justice, if so only can he clear the character of an innocent man.

In some of these cases the penance may be a condition of absolution, and the priest does not violate the seal if the penitent is willing that his sins should be thus made known.

XII

But let the priest observe diligently, when and to whom absolution should be granted or denied, and when it should be postponed; so that he may grant it in accordance with the rule to those who are duly disposed, and deny it to those who are not. Amongst the latter he must reckon those who give no signs of sorrow, who are unwilling to lay aside hatred and enmity, or to restore if they can other men's property, or to forsake the immediate occasion of sin, or in any other way abandon sin, or amend their life; or who have given public scandal, unless they make a public satisfaction and remove it.

The caution about public scandal is very necessary. Supposing a parish priest has duly warned a person not to approach the sacraments, especially if he is fortified by the authority of the Bishop, another priest, who hears the penitent's confession, has no right to remove the disciplinary bar without reference to the authority by whom it has been imposed.

XIII

Amongst those whose dispositions are doubtful habitual sinners must commonly be counted; and as a rule absolution should not be bestowed upon them apart from a case of necessity and without some marked improvement; especially if they have more than once broken faith previously given.

XIV

Let the priest remember not to impose upon the sick a weighty and laborious penance, but point out one, which they can accomplish in due time if they get well. In the meanwhile, having regard to the gravity of the disease, when some prayer and some little act of satisfaction has been imposed and accepted, let them be absolved, as need be.

XV

Moreover, besides the kindness, knowledge, and prudence required in confession, it is necessary also that he preserve the seal of secret confession inviolate, under exact and perpetual silence; so that he never says or does anything which either directly or indirectly tends to reveal any sin or defect known through confession alone. But neither let him presume to make use of any knowledge acquired in confession, to the hurt or danger of the penitent; neither let him speak even in a general way of sins heard in confession unless necessity demands it; and then discreetly and with great prudence, so that no suspicion, however slight, may arise about particular persons; nor let him even speak of them in the presence of laymen, lest they be offended.

The doctrine of the seal is of great importance. It is clearly taught in the 113th Canon (1603), which deals with the duty of presenting notorious evil livers:—

"Provided always, that if any man confess his secret and hidden sins to the minister, for the unburdening of his conscience, and to receive spiritual consolation and ease of mind from him; we do not in any way bind the said minister by this our Constitution, but do straitly charge and admonish him, that he do not at any time reveal and make known to any person whatsoever any crime or offence so committed to his trust and secrecy, (except they be such crimes as by the laws of this realm his own life may be called into question for concealing the same), under pain of irregularity."[1]

The observance of this rule requires constant watchfulness and a habit of reticence and discretion, which can only be attained by those who aim at a life of recollection and self-discipline. Where confession is voluntary, people will naturally abstain from it unless they are convinced that the priest to whom they resort would suffer anything rather than betray their confidence. It should be clearly recognised by clergy and laity alike that a priest is justified in denying, even on oath, that he knows anything against the character of a person, if his knowledge is derived only from the penitent's own confession.

This is an extreme step, which no conscientious priest would take without grave necessity, and it

[1] A valuable letter on the Privilege of Religious Confessions in English Courts of Justice, was published by Edward Badeley, barrister-at-law, in 1865 (Butterworth, London), in which he shows that the sanctity of the seal is and must be respected in the Law-courts. His conclusion is, "'Summa ratio est quæ pro religione facit,' is an old maxim of English law, and no person, I am satisfied, who knows anything of the subject, or considers it seriously, can reasonably doubt that the cause of religion is deeply interested in maintaining the sacred inviolability of confession."

is almost always possible to avoid placing one's self in a position from which there is no other way of escape.

A necessary corollary from this is that a priest should generally refuse to give letters testimonial to persons whose confessions he hears. In nine cases out of ten, no doubt, he could do so without difficulty; in the tenth case he must either refuse, which in an isolated case would arouse suspicion, or else he must suppress the fact damaging to the penitent that he knows, and yet must not tell.

The Roman Catholic manuals give many stories to illustrate the danger of an inexperienced confessor breaking the seal, by careless reference to things which he has heard in confession.

Perhaps it is only right to add that there is a widespread feeling that married priests are less trustworthy as confessors than celibates. The present writer has no reason to suppose that this is the case, but it is obvious that special care is needed to give no cause for the suspicion that the secrets of the confessional are endangered by family life and social intercourse.

VI

THE ORDINARY USE OF CONFESSION

There are three occasions in the ordinary ministry of the parish priest, when he is bound, in loyalty to the Book of Common Prayer, to give his people the opportunity of confession, and even in some cases to urge it on them: when he prepares candidates for Confirmation, when he visits the sick and dying, and when he gives formal notice of Holy Communion —as, for instance, before a great festival.

(i.) As regards Confirmation, it is clearly the duty of the priest to see that his candidates are duly instructed in all that concerns the life of penitence and faith; and moreover, the Bishop's prayer for the sevenfold gifts of the Holy Ghost implies that the candidates have received the gift of regeneration by water and the Holy Ghost, *and the forgiveness of all their sins.*

I do not desire to insist that the candidate must have received a special sacramental absolution just before his Confirmation, but at least he is supposed to be in a state of grace, enjoying the blessings of pardon and peace.

It is difficult to see how any candidate can be properly prepared until he has been taught to examine his conscience, and make a real confession of his sins to God. Sometimes the private confession of sin to God will suffice, but in many cases confession to God in the presence of a priest will add seriousness to the repentance, and secure that real assurance of forgiveness which would otherwise be lacking. Moreover, in the case of young people who have lived sheltered lives, and are presumably free from any serious sin, though they do not need to use it at the moment, to learn what confession means will be of immense value to them in the future, when more urgent occasion for its use will probably arise.

Here the question may be raised whether children and young persons should be encouraged or permitted to make their confession without their parents' consent. Many would say "Certainly not," and it is clearly right that the practice should not become habitual without the knowledge of the parents, but it would not be safe to say that in no case should a priest hear the confession of a child until the parents' permission has been given. Such a rule might deprive the child of his best chance of escape from terrible sin. It often happens that a young girl is in serious trouble. She opens her grief in confession, and a wise priest tells her that it is her duty to let her mother know what is the matter, and get the advice and protection that she needs. In such cases the mother is often very grateful to the priest, though perhaps, if she had been asked beforehand whether she wished her child to make a confession, she would have said "No"; because she had no idea what it really meant, or how greatly her child needed it.

On the other hand, there is a serious danger of encouraging young people to make their confession as a matter of course, and because others are doing so. Where the practice becomes quite common, we should take pains to insist that confession must be entirely voluntary, and that the child fully realises the sinfulness of making an unreal or untrue confession.

Again, it is not generally wise to encourage children and young people to make their confessions at regular or frequent intervals, and certainly not before each Communion. Such a method may have apparent advantages for the time. The priest is encouraged by seeing his catechumens come quite regularly, but in the long run the results are disappointing. Where the young communicants are entirely dependent on a particular priest, there may be no spontaneous spiritual life, and no independent growth in grace. If they are removed from the particular influence, they are in danger of not taking pains to prepare themselves, and so are likely to drift away from Holy Communion altogether. It is surely better that they should be taught to examine their own consciences, and encouraged to come to Holy Communion with growing frequency, as they desire it, provided they are free from deadly sin. That is the teaching of S. Augustine, to which he refers again and again. In the "Sermon to Catechumens" he says:—

"When you have been baptized, hold fast to a good life in the commandments of GOD, that you may preserve your baptism to the end. I do not say that you can live here without sin, but those are venial sins, without which this life cannot be. Baptism is found to be the remedy for all sin; for little sins, which we cannot be without, the remedy is prayer. In Baptism we are washed once for all, day by day we are washed in prayer. But never commit those sins for which it is necessary that you should be cut off from the body of Christ; far be that from you. Those whom you see doing penance have committed crimes, adulteries, or some outrageous deeds; hence they are doing penance. For if their sins had been slight, daily prayer would have sufficed to blot them out."[1]

S. Augustine, of course, is speaking here of doing

[1] The "Sermo ad Catechumenos" was probably preached A.D. 400, and is given in Heurtley's *De Fide et Symbolo.*

public penance, but that makes no difference to the point that venial sins are remitted in answer to prayer alone. Elsewhere he says that the recitation of the "Our Father" is sufficient.

We may fully admit that good people, living strict and holy lives, may use the sacrament of penance, if they desire to do so, as a means of discipline; but that is a very different matter from insisting on, or even encouraging, its very frequent use by young people.

On the other hand, while one would discourage the frequent and regular confessions of children, they cannot be too clearly taught that it is the natural and appropriate remedy for the serious sins, into which even quite young boys and girls may easily fall.

It is indeed a lamentable fact that, under the ordinary methods which prevail in the Church of England, a very large proportion of our young communicants drift away. Here is a typical case. A young man is confirmed and makes his first Communion, and perhaps goes on steadily and well for months, or even years. Then he falls into a serious sin, which his conscience tells him is quite inconsistent with the life of a communicant. He stays away from Communion. Too often his absence is unnoticed, and nothing is said to encourage him to return; but the incompetent or careless priest may do worse than ignore his absence. Sometimes, without taking into account that the young man probably has only too good a reason for refraining from Communion, the priest merely urges him to return, for he forgets that practical compulsion to Communion is far more dangerous than compulsion to confession. If the young man is honest and sincere, he is shocked at the shallowness of a priest who apparently only desires to keep up the number of his communicants; if he is weak or insincere, he returns to Communion without any real repentance, and to the permanent injury of his conscience.

How different the effect would be if the priest, while expressing his real sorrow for the young man's absence, invited him to come and prepare by a good confession. That would help him to regain the ground which he had lost, and enable him to realise at once the seriousness of sin and the reality of pardon. It is indeed sad that for lack of such an obvious remedy many young people should drift away, after a single false step, into the vast army of the self-excommunicated. But the young man may have abstained from Holy Communion, not because he has really fallen into deadly sin; it may be only a scruple that keeps him back, which will be readily removed if he comes to open his grief, and finds a sympathetic and discerning priest.

Another question arises with reference to the

confessions of young people. The present writer advises that candidates should normally be encouraged to make a sacramental confession on the eve of Confirmation, provided that there is no sort of compulsion, and that everything is done to produce real contrition, because the experience of a first confession will make it easy to return if afterwards they fall away; but confession should not normally be separated by any long interval from Holy Communion. Strictly speaking, absolution is not so much a separate sacrament, conferring a special grace of its own, as it is the removal of the barrier between the soul and GOD, and the readmission to the full privilege of Communion.

If this is so, there can be no reason for granting absolution and yet withholding Communion. It may be, of course, that Communion is rightly delayed, because a further time is needed to test the reality of the penitence, or to avoid scandal. For instance, it may be a wise rule in a penitentiary not to allow a penitent to receive her Communion until she has been an inmate for twelve months; but where that rule exists, she ought not to receive absolution until she is ready for Communion. Meanwhile, she may be assured that the withholding of absolution for a time does not mean that GOD has not forgiven her. She is kept waiting, not for Divine forgiveness, but for the sacramental seal of forgiveness, which admits her to the Eucharistic Feast.

So as regards young children not yet ready to be confirmed. The ideal person to hear their confessions is the father or the mother. The priest who wins their confidence may stand *in loco parentis*, and a child may make a very real and true confession, but he should not be taught to expect or desire absolution until the time has come for Confirmation and Communion. The wise parent will, in some serious cases, encourage the child to go to God's Minister for an informal, or even a formal, confession.

Many priests who agree with the writer that it is desirable that their Confirmation candidates should be led to make their confessions, if it can be done without any sort of compulsion, complain that in fact very few of them are willing to accept the invitation. One has often heard priests say, "I always have a private interview with each candidate, and offer to receive his confession, but I get little or no response."

I venture to suggest that this comes from a faulty method of preparation. So long as the candidates are instructed in classes, and the priest never comes to close quarters with the candidate till the final interview, he should not be surprised if the candidate is much too shy to think of confession. The instructions may have been excellent in themselves, and yet the candidates have not taken them in. There is many a slip betwixt cup and lip, and many a true word from the lips of a teacher never reaches the ear, much less the heart, of his hearers.

The merely intellectual results are far more satisfactory when the lessons are imparted to individual candidates one by one, and the priest who has taught his candidate, not once or twice, but ten or twelve times in a private interview, has probably broken down the barrier of shyness. The earlier interviews have been largely occupied in hearing repetition of the Catechism or other doctrinal lessons, and in looking over written work; and then, when the time comes to stir the conscience, and give practical help about private prayer and private penitence, the candidate is thankful to tell out his troubles and his sins.

No doubt this method takes time, but there is no time better spent, and if only the clergy would abandon the management of clubs and nine-tenths of the trivialities which are dignified with the name of parochial work, they would find time enough for the highest and most fruitful part of their ministry. With a careful management of his time—if he is willing, for instance, to give up five or six consecutive hours on Saturday afternoon and evening[1]—the parish priest may make his preparation of candidates for Confirmation of infinitely greater value.

[1] Such was the practice of the late Canon Brooke of S. John's, Kennington.

(ii.) To adopt the individual method of preparing for Confirmation may seem to some an innovation, but there is certainly nothing new in the suggestion that the visitation of the sick and dying is the special opportunity for putting before individuals the duty and privilege of private confession.

It has been suggested that the Order for the Visitation of the Sick needs revision. We need some provision for the due administration of the ancient and scriptural sacrament of Holy Unction, considered not as a preparation for death, but as the appropriate accompaniment of special prayer for bodily health. We need, no doubt, additional prayers for the recovery of health, as well as for resignation and the right use of sickness; but the revision of the Prayer-book is of much less importance than the thorough use of the Prayer-book as it is. How very different the state of religion in England would be if the clergy really carried out the intentions of the Church. The solemn Office of the Visitation of the Sick has often been abandoned for a method, which satisfies a vague religious sentiment, while it drugs the conscience and leaves the soul to face the Day of Judgment, "unhouseled, disappointed, unanealed."

The following rubric demands nothing less than a real probing of the conscience:—

Then shall the Minister examine whether he repent him truly of his sins, and be in charity with all the world; exhorting him to forgive from the bottom of his heart all persons that have offended him, and if he hath offended any other, to ask their forgiveness, and when he hath done injury or wrong to any man, that he makes amends to the utmost of his power.

Here shall the sick person be moved to make a special confession of his sins, if he feel his conscience troubled with any weighty matter. After which confession the priest shall absolve him (if he humbly and heartily desire it) after this sort.

Then follows the prescribed form of absolution, which is applicable to those who are sick both in body and soul, and to those who, though in sound bodily health, are conscious of the sickness of the soul. No wonder that the work of the Church is shallow and ineffectual, if a large proportion of the clergy must admit that they have never moved any one, sick or whole, to make a special confession of his sin, and have never used the words of absolution.

(iii.) But we can hardly expect that the sick will "humbly and heartily desire" the absolution, if it has not been put before them as part of the ordinary ministry of the Church.

There may be good reason for curtailing, or even omitting altogether on ordinary occasions, the long exhortation which the minister is ordered to use on every Sunday when he gives warning for the celebration of the Holy Communion, but it is difficult to conceive any adequate excuse for neglecting it before the great festivals. Three times a year at least the priest should remind his flock of the blessings of Communion, of the great peril of unworthily receiving, and of the means of preparing for it. While he is bound to charge intending communicants with the duty of "searching their own consciences," and while he must acknowledge that in some cases nothing more is needed, yet the invitation to confession must be given.

Because it is requisite, that no man should come to the Holy Communion, but with a full trust in God's mercy, and with a quiet conscience; therefore, if there be any of you by this means cannot quiet his own conscience herein, but requireth further comfort or counsel, let him come to me, or to some other discreet and learned Minister of God's Word, and open his grief; that by the ministry of God's holy Word he may receive the benefit of absolution, together with ghostly counsel and advice, to the quieting of his conscience, and avoiding of all scruple and doubtfulness.

Enough has been said to show that in the ordinary ministration of the parish priest, in the instruction of candidates for Confirmation, in the visitation of the sick, and in the public notice of Holy Communion, there are abundant opportunities of inculcating the use of confession, and where confession is unknown, we can only conclude that the ordinary ministry of the parish priest has been wanting in courage, or in loyalty to the system of the Church.

To recover ground that has been lost, and to recall the minds of priests and people to the ideals of the Church, something more is needed, and in the following chapter some account will be given of the way in which a special parochial mission may serve to introduce a deeper penitence, and a fuller realisation of the value of confession.

VII

PAROCHIAL MISSIONS

In the previous chapter I have tried to show how the ordinary ministry of the parish priest must include the teaching and practice of confession, if he makes a serious attempt to carry out the system of the Church; but when the teaching of the Church has been obscured, partly by mere neglect, and partly by the intrusion of an alien tradition, something more than ordinary parochial work is needed to recover what has been lost.

The Church in England is still affected very largely by two influences, which are injurious to her true position as an integral part of the Catholic Church, if indeed she claims to hold primitive and apostolic doctrine, and to protest only against what is false.

Since the Reformation, the connection between Church and State, with its roots in the distant past, has generally fostered the growth of worldliness, and a type of semi-religious life which shrinks from discipline and the doctrine of the Cross. The attempt to identify the Church and the nation has led to the degradation of the two great sacraments, and has undermined belief in the authority of the priesthood and the reality of sacramental grace.

These consequences of "Establishment" have been lately exposed with just severity in the Bampton Lectures of Canon Hobhouse.[1]

After the degradation of the Church and its work in the Hanoverian period, and until the rise of the Oxford Tractarians, the saving salt, which preserved the Church from the total loss of spiritual character, was chiefly supplied by the Evangelical Movement. In their loyalty to Jesus Christ, in their zeal for personal holiness, in their protest against worldliness and sin, the Evangelical leaders largely counteracted the secularity which would otherwise have paralysed the Church, but their religious system was in some respects an alien tradition, which generally ignored, and sometimes deliberately contradicted, the sacramental system.

While they rightly insisted on the need of conversion, and emphasised the personal relation between the soul and the Saviour, the Evangelical leaders made little or nothing of the Church, and regarded Baptism and the Holy Eucharist as by no means essential.

Seventy years ago the Oxford leaders made their

[1] *The Church and the World in Idea and History.*

protest, and in spite of ceaseless opposition there has been a marvellous recovery of the true idea of the Church and of the sacramental life; but there are still vast areas in which the Erastian spirit, or the Evangelical tradition, or a curious mixture of the two, hold the field.

If he is to build up the lives of his flock on the lines of the Prayer-book, the parish priest feels the need of some strong spiritual reinforcement. Under favourable conditions this may be supplied by a parochial mission, and in this chapter an attempt must be made to show how a mission often enables priest and people to start fresh on the sounder lines of genuine Churchmanship.

This is not the place to enlarge on the history of parochial missions as they have been known in England during the past fifty years. They have been largely used by two out of the three schools of thought which exist in the Church of England to-day. Broad Churchmen are too academic in their tastes, and too hazy in their beliefs to claim much share in parochial missions; if they have taken any part, it has not been on lines of their own, but in a temporary and rather unreal alliance with one of the other schools of thought. To Evangelicals the idea of parochial missions has been congenial from the first, and they have thrown themselves into the work with energy and enthusiasm. The older generation of Tractarians held aloof, shrinking from methods which seemed so unlike the sober ways associated with the best Anglican traditions, as they were exhibited by John Keble in the poetry of the *Christian Year* and in his own life.

The suspicion that missions were incompatible with Church order has been gradually laid aside. When men like Father Benson and Father O'Neil of Cowley threw themselves heartily into the great London Mission in 1874, they brought the knowledge and experience of Catholic faith and practice to meet the zeal of the Evangelicals, and gradually a school of missioners grew up, who learned to use to the full the strength derived from this happy alliance.

It is not too much to say that in the gradual evolution of the modern parochial mission the Evangelical fervour has been retained, while the sensational elements have been discarded, and the main stress has been laid on careful and systematic teaching.

Missions which are purely emotional have been discredited, because experience has shown that the apparent results quickly evaporate, and when the first enthusiasm dies down the parish is left in the condition of an extinct volcano.

This is now recognised by Churchmen of all schools of thought, and the element of instruction has largely increased. Very frequent, if not daily, celebrations of the Holy Communion are held in the missions conducted by those, who are described as Evangelical, if not Low Church, and their missions encourage much more definite adhesion to Church doctrine than was formerly the case. The writer's own experience lies chiefly in missions, where parish priest and missioner alike desire that souls, who are converted to God, shall have the opportunity of making a very real and definite confession of sin. He would not say that the value of a mission may be measured by the number of those who make their confessions in the presence of a priest, but he is confident that missions ought to have the result of bringing the parish priest and his people so near together, that the practice of confession comes to be regarded as natural and right.

It may be of some service to explain how this result can be attained. Of course a mission is an exceptional spiritual enterprise, and ought not to be attempted without weeks or months of prayerful preparation. Its results depend not on the magnetic power of the preacher, nor on the elaborate organisation of the parish, but on the presence and power of the Holy Ghost. It is in humble dependence on Him that every effort is made to bring sinners to repentance. The Love of God revealed in the Incarnation, the Passion, the Resurrection of our Lord is set before men's minds; the nature and effects of sin are clearly described; and the result is seen in a serious concern about spiritual things such as is scarcely ever perceived at any other time. It is when men and women are pricked to the heart, and crying out for definite instruction, that the missioner is bound to tell them plainly of the divinely appointed remedy for sin. It would be cruel to conceal the fact that our Lord Jesus "hath given power and commandment to His Ministers to declare and pronounce to His people being penitent the absolution and remission of their sins."

The moment comes when the most unlikely people welcome the message of pardon and peace, which at ordinary times seems so remote from their spiritual experience.

If the missioner utterly disregards the counsels showered upon him to be "moderate and safe," and is simply possessed with the longing to save souls from sin, his ministry cannot but secure conversions, which gladden the angels and leave the human messenger humbled in the dust, yet supremely thankful that God can use weak and sinful men to achieve so much.

The kind of mission, then, which the writer ventures to recommend is an attempt to combine and utilise two converging lines of thought. The zeal of the evangelist is tempered by the knowledge and the discipline of the Catholic tradition. He distrusts mere excitement; he will not be satisfied if he fills the Church with those who find little or nothing in his preaching, which differs from that of the Methodist, or of such great revivalists as Messrs. Moody and Sankey. While he recognises that their work is mainly good, and true so far as it goes, he is deeply conscious that something more is needed. The awakened sinner must be clearly shown that conversion is the beginning, not the end, of true Christian life.

With this ideal kept steadily in view the missioner's sermons and instructions are not merely a series of repeated efforts to touch the heart and bend the will; they are the attempt to present great truths in an orderly sequence, and they follow with more or less exactness the order of the spiritual exercises which are generally attributed to Ignatius of Loyola, but which were in use long before his time.[1]

This has been the method of a large and increasing school of missioners in England ever since the first great London Mission held in 1874, and there has been gradually evolved a scientific method in missions which makes the work far more telling. There is no need to insist that well-conducted missions invigorate parochial life in many other directions, for the object of the present chapter is to show how the missioner

[1] See the *Spiritual Exercises* of Cisneros, a Spanish Benedictine born half a century before Ignatius.

can help the parish priest to get the ministry of absolution recognised and used. When the foundations have been duly laid, and conviction of sin is reached, the missioner teaches plainly the duty of self-examination, and insists that none will profit by the mission who do not try to face the fact of personal sin. He is able sometimes to reach the conscience by speaking about certain common sins more plainly than is possible for the parish priest in his ordinary ministry. He recommends to all who are in earnest the use of forms of self-examination, which not only bring to light hidden sins but suggest a higher standard of moral and spiritual effort. In very many cases men and women, who take him at his word, are so deeply conscious of their need that they drink in readily the instruction, which follows later, on the ministry of absolution.

The missioner, of course, has nothing new to say. He only repeats the teaching which the parish priest ought to have given long before, or which he has given without, in fact, reaching the hearts of his people. He has no need to add anything to the teaching of the Book of Common Prayer, and he has no difficulty in showing how that is consistent with Holy Scripture and with common sense.

The result is that during the mission many will avail themselves of the opportunity of making a first confession. It may never need to be repeated.

Souls restored to the life of grace will only need to persevere in the life of prayer and communion, with continual meditation on the Word of God, but the experience of the mission and their first confession can never be forgotten. If unhappily there comes a relapse into serious sin, they know now where to find the remedy.

Others will desire to make confessions in the future with more or less of frequency and regularity. If the parish priest is in full sympathy with the teaching of the mission, and *himself a penitent*, he will find that the way is open now to make confession a recognised, and very important, part of his ordinary ministry.

Much more might be said on the general subject of the value of parochial missions in promoting a deeper penitence, and a higher standard of devotion, but rather than attempt to repeat what has been well said by others I will only refer to the *Missioner's Handbook* by my brother Paul Bull (Grant Richards, 1904).

I may be allowed to quote what he has said with characteristic vigour.

"If the parish priest has instructed his people faithfully in the doctrine and discipline of the Church, every communicant will know that he is free to make a special confession of his sins, if his conscience is troubled. But this liberty is seldom realised. Strong prejudice, persistent misrepresentation, and falsehood have blinded people's minds to the clear teaching of the English Church on this matter. . . .

"Teaching on confession should be clear, downright, and definite; the evasive and apologetic way in which this matter of Church discipline has been taught only arouses a natural suspicion; absolute openness and frankness are necessary. . . .

"This form of confession is a recognition of our corporate responsibility—that sin injures the whole Communion of Saints, the Church, the family of GOD, and therefore GOD bestows His pardon through that Body. It ensures a careful self-examination, and helps to a more full self-knowledge; it humbles that false pride which is the root of all sin; it ensures experienced counsel; it affords strong support in times of temptation; it saves many souls from that stagnation of the spiritual life which does not strive after entire self-conquest, or aim at perfection; it tests the reality of repentance by submitting it to the judgment of another person; and it satisfies a deep instinct of healthy human nature, which cannot bear to conceal sin, but longs to unbosom itself, and to be known for what it really is" (pp. 169–171).

VIII

THE FORM OF CONFESSION

THE use of a definite form of confession helps to bring out the truth that confession should be made to GOD. The priest is only the witness and the minister of a gift which comes from the one and only fountain of mercy. This truth is sometimes distorted and sometimes forgotten. A great deal of prejudice against confession is due to the fact that people have imagined that confession to a priest is taught as an alternative to confession to Almighty GOD. The idea is of course preposterous. The priest has no power of a merely personal sort; he is only the channel through which the blessing comes; and this is why we emphasise the sacramental character of the whole transaction. If on the one hand the position of the priest has been distorted by exaggerating his powers; on the other hand the true idea of confession is forgotten, if the priest is regarded merely as a friend who offers advice and sympathy. No doubt the confidential talks which take place between a pastor and members of his flock, who come to him privately, have a very real value of their own. As they sit beside the study fire hearts are opened and tongues are loosed, and if the pastor is sympathetic he hears a good deal of autobiographical matter, in which some genuine confession of sin is mixed up with a good deal of self-pity or self-praise.

The situation is completely changed, and changed for the better, if the priest is led to say, "Shall we not try to disentangle your own wrong-doing from the things which you could not help? Perhaps your doubts and perplexities, your clouded faith, and your general distress are due to the fact of sin. Will you not come with me to church, either now or when you have taken more time to think and pray about it? Yours is a case for confession, *not to man but to God.*" If the man has faith and courage enough for this, the confession that he makes in church will be more real and searching in its self-accusation, and the priest, when he has assumed his spiritual office, will gently but decisively forbid the excuses and the palliatives which were tolerable enough in merely friendly conversation. The utter sincerity which this kind of confession demands is made easier for both penitent and priest by the knowledge that all which passes is under the sacramental seal. The penitent knows that the priest is bound to secrecy so absolute, that he must not refer to the matter again even to the penitent himself without his permission.

In order to emphasise the distinction between a friendly conversation and a very solemn religious act, it is generally expedient that the priest should wear a surplice and a stole.

This is specially important when the penitent is a woman. The kind of confidential talks in his study to which the priest naturally invites the men and boys are eminently undesirable for the other sex. If a woman wishes to disclose her secret sins, the church is the only place where she can do so with propriety, unless it is a case of serious illness, in which the priest must if necessary hear confessions in a sick room. In either case the woman will naturally desire that the dress and demeanour of the priest shall make plain the sacred, and ministerial, nature of his office.

The sacramental character of the confession, its reference to Almighty God, is preserved by the use of a traditional form. It may be well to quote here a form in common use without claiming any special authority for it.

When the penitent has knelt down, and perhaps asked for a special blessing, the priest says:—

"May the Lord be in thy heart and on thy lips, that thou mayest faithfully and fully confess thy sins unto Him."

Then the penitent begins:—

"I confess to God the Father Almighty, to His only-begotten Son Jesus Christ our Lord, to God the Holy Ghost, before the whole Company of Heaven, and before thee, my father, that I have sinned exceedingly in thought, word, and deed, through my own fault, through my own most grievous fault. (Since my last confession) I have sinned (here follows the particular confession) . . . For these and all my other sins which I cannot now remember I am heartily sorry, firmly purpose amendment, and humbly ask pardon of Almighty God, and of you, my father, penance, counsel, and absolution. Wherefore I pray God the Father Almighty, His only-begotten Son Jesus Christ our Lord, and God the Holy Ghost to have mercy upon me, and thee, father, to pray to the Lord our God for me. Amen."

The form raises several questions, some of which have been discussed already, and some of which call for further exposition.

We notice that the confession is made to God, and that there is a distinct recognition of the Communion of Saints. Sometimes this is emphasised as in the ancient formula by adding after the mention of the Blessed Trinity "to Blessed Mary and all the Saints," but in the judgment of the present writer, it is better not to use language which is easily misunderstood, and apparently goes beyond the limits of the Book of Common Prayer.

It is right that the priest should be addressed as a spiritual father, for the term is the natural expression of the relation thus established, but if the penitent prefers to say "and before you His minister," the priest should be quite content. The title of father should be gratefully and humbly accepted, but not demanded as a right. Again, if the words which express contrition seem too strong, as going beyond the spiritual experience of the penitent, it is well that he should substitute others which seem more real and true. Many persons are relieved if they are taught to say, "For these and all my other sins I am sorry, and pray that I may be more sorry than I am."

Next comes the more serious question whether the penitent is bound to confess all his sins. It is sometimes pointed out that the Prayer-book suggests not the detailed enumeration of all his sins, but the acknowledgment of some single weighty matter. The question looms larger in controversial writings than in actual practice.

Strictly speaking, even on the Roman Catholic theory it is only necessary to confess deadly sins; and it is obviously impossible for any one to confess all his sins. But the sinner who is really penitent, and desires to tell out honestly the chief matters that trouble his conscience, is generally quite willing and anxious to confess all his other sins so far as he knows them. If he only wishes to disclose a single sin without any attempt to make a full confession of all the rest, he is quite free to do so. It may relieve his conscience and enable him to get advice, but he is not entitled to absolution. When people ask for absolution for a single sin, they show a misconception of the whole meaning of Divine forgiveness. God does not forgive first one sin and then another; He forgives not the sins but the sinner; and the sinner is only capable of receiving forgiveness when he is prepared to confess and forsake all his sins so far as he can. The assurance of Divine forgiveness may indeed be otherwise obtained, but if it is to reach the sinner through the lips of the priest, the latter must know the nature of the sins committed.

Moreover, it must be clearly recognised that no confession is really complete. "Who can tell how oft he offendeth?" "My sins are more in number than the hairs of my head." Every true penitent knows that. He can but do his best; but it would, of course, render the confession null and void if the penitent wilfully concealed any grave sin, or circumstance which rendered a sin confessed still graver than it seemed. That is why the priest is sometimes obliged to ask questions, *e.g.* "Does the sin concern others besides yourself? Is it a matter in which reparation is due? Are you in danger of falling again into the same sin? Are you willing to make restitution, and to avoid the occasion of sin in the future?"

Some of these points must be discussed still further, but here it is only necessary to say that if a man desires absolution he must make a full confession of all grave sins committed since his Baptism, or since his last confession, so far as he is able to do so. For instance, if he has lived in habitual disregard of the duties of public worship and of private prayer he should say for how long a time that has lasted. If he has been dishonest he must acknowledge the full extent of the wrong he has done, and be ready to restore to the utmost of his power. If he has injured another by robbing him or her of innocence, or in any way making another the accomplice of his sin, there are very definite ways of proving the reality of his penitence. Of these things the priest cannot judge unless the whole case is laid before him. The pronouncing of the absolution is not a mere form, but the expression of a deliberate judgment on facts, known with all the accuracy that is possible.

When the penitent has made his confession as fully and honestly as he can, he is always taught to add, "For these and all my other sins which I know not of, and which I cannot now remember, I am heartily sorry," &c., and he must be assured that the absolution covers everything.

This is really important, for some persons after a first confession are troubled by the notion that they have left out sins, which should have been confessed. They should be well assured that if they did their best, and honestly confessed whatever grave sins were before their mind, they were fully forgiven, and to go back upon the past would be to doubt the love of God, and the power of His redeeming grace.

It is possible that under special circumstances and at very rare intervals it may be permissible to repeat a general confession; but the desire to do so is generally the indication of a morbid and over-scrupulous conscience. A wise confessor will not exactly forbid his penitent to make a general confession; he will rather try to lead him into a fuller trust, and a larger sense of the liberty wherewith Christ has made His people free, encouraging not morbid introspection, but rather the spirit of praise and thanksgiving.

The form reminds us further that the penitent is expected to ask for penance and advice, as well as absolution, and sometimes it is necessary to explain the terms. He should ask for penance, because he owns that his sin deserves punishment, and even when God freely forgives sin He does not remit the punishment. It was so in the case of David. Nathan heard his confession and pronounced his absolution. He was commissioned to say, "The Lord hath put away thy sin, thou shalt not die," but he was obliged to tell him that punishment would follow. "Howbeit because by this deed thou hast given great occasion to the enemies of the Lord to blaspheme, the child also that is born unto thee shall die" (2 Sam. xii. 13, 14).

Sometimes the penitent needs to be reminded that the worst consequence of sin is separation from God. The absolution is the pledge and guarantee that this is at an end; but the minor consequences remain. Forgiveness does not mean that the sinner is restored to the position in which he might have been, had he never sinned. The man who has shattered his health and dissipated his fortune by intemperance may be forgiven at the very moment of his turning to God, but a large measure of suffering and loss remains. The true penitent is glad to bear it. He knows that it is his due. Over and above these natural consequences of sin which remain, and which we may describe as the penance exacted by God Himself, it is customary to impose some act of penance, which the penitent will perform in token of his gratitude to God and submission to the discipline of His Church.

Generally the penance imposed is something very slight, such as the saying once or twice of a penitential psalm, some special abstinence, or some act of devotion. It is better that this should be kept quite distinct from the course of conduct recommended, as a means of self-discipline or as aid to spiritual advance, or from the acts of reparation and restitution which must be performed, or promised, before absolution can be pronounced. It is surely quite wrong to prescribe as a penance something, which ought to form a normal part of daily life in Christ.

When there is a danger of the doctrine of penance being misunderstood, and even allowed to obscure the truth that there is no sacrifice or satisfaction for sin but in the Cross, it is better to assign no penance, but to excite the gratitude and love of the penitent by pointing to the fulness and freedom of the Divine gift of pardon.

So again the penitent is taught to ask for counsel, but it does not follow that the priest should give it. It may be that he is entirely without the knowledge or experience which would entitle him to offer counsel to one far more advanced than himself in spiritual things. He may realise that his penitent has really come for absolution only, and that he needs no other guidance than that of the Holy Ghost. An inexperienced confessor sometimes wearies the penitent, and wastes time, by offering advice which is not needed or desired.

A penitent is in no way bound to place himself under the direction and guidance of a confessor, whom he approaches only for the sake of absolution, and the priest must be careful not to assume more authority than is necessary.

Finally, it is remarkable that some people come to confession without any definite idea of seeking absolution. The longing to unburden one's self is often strongly felt, where there is no appreciation of the truth that God has commissioned His Church to absolve in His Name. The Prayer-book reminds us that absolution is not to be given where it is not asked for—the priest shall absolve him *if he humbly and heartily desire it.*

The desire for absolution will not be felt until there is a lively faith in the reality of Christ's presence with His Church, manifest in the sacramental system as the extension of His Incarnate life; but the priest who has before him a sinner, so convinced of sin that he is willing to make a full and true confession, will have no difficulty in showing that the word of absolution, pronounced by God Himself through human lips, is precisely the blessing that he needs.

IX

ON WITHHOLDING ABSOLUTION

AMONG the Latin Rules quoted in Chapter V., No. XII. reminds us of the difficulty of determining when absolution should be refused or delayed. Where confessions are very rarely made, it may be generally assumed that no one comes unless he is really penitent and therefore capable of receiving absolution, but there are now some parishes where the practice of confession is so thoroughly established, that there is a real danger lest, amidst a crowd of serious and well-disposed penitents, there may be some who have come with a light heart, and with no real intention of forsaking sin and turning to GOD.

Priests in the Church of England are spared from the very painful duty of receiving irreligious and worldly people, who are driven to confession by the pressure of public opinion, or by a rule from which they cannot escape without renouncing all definite membership in the Church. Our people are not obliged to come if they wish to be married in Church, and to receive Christian burial. Yet we too are tempted to lower the standard; to cry "Peace, peace" where there is no peace, and to "heal the hurt of God's people lightly" (Jer. vi. 14). Some will come to confession because they find it easier to put their trust in a priest than to examine their own conscience and make a real break with sin. In view of this very real danger we must lay to heart the words—

> "If censure sleep will absolution hold?
> Will God affirm their acts of grace
> Who never dare deny?"

In each case the confessor must be satisfied that the confession is as honest and complete as the penitent can make it; that there is a real turning to God; that he is ready to make whatever restitution is possible; and that there is a full purpose of amendment. Let us consider some typical cases. A man may come with his conscience seriously troubled by some definite breach of the Seventh or Eighth Commandment, but not conscious of the gravity of other sins. He may, for instance, have lived in the habitual neglect of public worship and of private prayer. Surely he ought not to be absolved unless he intends for the future to fulfil the ordinary and elementary duties of the Christian life. He is not fit for absolution and Communion if he has no definite intention of living a Christian life. In a subsequent chapter something must be said as to the rule of life which should be suggested, but here we need only remark that the confessor must often point out that the breaches of the Second Table, which trouble the conscience, are really due to something more fundamental. The sinner has got wrong with God, and needs nothing less than a thorough conversion.

Again, a young person may come to confession, and while acknowledging other sins may be almost unconscious of the gravity of his or her offences against the Fifth Commandment. The confessor must do his best to re-establish right relations in the home, and he must insist that duty to God and to His Church can be harmonised with duty to parents. Carelessness in this respect, and failure to support the legitimate authority of parents, has been the cause of much prejudice against confession, and has encouraged young people to imagine that they can substitute the authority of an indulgent spiritual father for that of an exacting parent.

Under the head of the Sixth Commandment very grave questions sometimes perplex the confessor. A murderer cannot rest without relieving his conscience of its awful burden, and the priest has to share his secret. There is, of course, no question of betraying the seal. The priest must at all costs preserve silence, but he has to advise the penitent and to grant or withhold absolution. If the life or liberty of another is at stake the murderer must be encouraged to give himself up to justice, and until he does so cannot be absolved.

Perhaps the penitent has already been tried and acquitted, or the fact, that a murder was committed, has never been detected. In that case the murderer is not bound to incriminate himself, but he is bound to make all possible reparation, and he must be encouraged to bear whatever pain and grief God lays upon him.

Under the Seventh Commandment questions sometimes arise which are painful and cannot be touched without grave peril to penitent and priest, but it is unnecessary and unwise to go into the minute details which are discussed *ad nauseam* in some Roman Catholic text-books and by some Protestant controversialists, who seem to take a very unwholesome delight in stirring up mud.

The priest must be specially on his guard, and I would refer again to Dr. Pusey's caution, quoted in Chapter I.

If husband or wife confess to a definite breach of the marriage vow, it is generally right to recommend that the sin be confessed to the injured partner, on the ground that there can be no real happiness in married life if there are secrets between the two. If the wife's sin has led to imposing on her husband another man's child, the obligation to confess it is the greater, especially if questions not only of maintenance but of inheritance are involved.

There are many cases in which one would not be justified in insisting on this confession, and it should seldom if ever be made a condition of absolution.

In all cases where sins against purity are confessed in which other persons are concerned, absolution should not be given unless there is a definite promise to avoid occasions of sin; and the priest must know exactly where the danger lies, in order that he may be satisfied of the penitent's intention to take real measures to avoid recurrence. There are cases in which reparation or restitution is due. Sometimes a man may be encouraged to marry the woman he has wronged, and he is bound to make provision for her child.

If married people confess any wilful violations of the ends for which Holy Matrimony was ordained they must be induced to aim at the highest standard, and their attention should be called to the grave dangers which attend the attempt to evade their natural responsibility.[1]

When personal sins which concern no one but the penitent are confessed, the priest must help him to distinguish between wilful and deliberate wrong-

[1] See a paper on the Declining Birth-rate by the late Dr. Taylor of Birmingham. London: Bailliere, Tindall & Co., Henrietta Street, Covent Garden.

doing and sinful thoughts, which may be regarded as temptation rather than sin, provided that there is no assent of the will

Sometimes in dealing with young men and boys it is necessary for the priest to give the kind of advice which should have been given by a father or mother, and, if young women and girls need counsel on matters of personal purity, they should be referred to a competent adviser of their own sex.

It is specially necessary, in dealing with sins against the Seventh Commandment, to show that the root of sins, which cause such special shame, is neglect of GOD. We must insist on the golden rule, "Walk in the Spirit and ye shall not fulfil the lusts of the flesh."

Under the Seventh Commandment a word must be added about intemperance in meat and drink. Sometimes the penitent must be shown that the other difficulties of which he complains are largely due to the fact that he has not learned to bridle his appetite, and that the sins against purity are the result of luxurious living. The duty of fasting and abstinence depends not only on the precept of the Church, but on the practical necessity of keeping under the body.

The penitent who confesses to habitual drunkenness should be strongly urged to total abstinence, and in some cases this may be even made a condition of absolution. One cannot be satisfied that a man is really penitent about his intemperance unless he is willing to make some very definite promise to guard against the occasion of it.

Under the Eighth Commandment the question of restitution is prominent, and the duty of the confessor is generally clear. If the penitent has been guilty of direct dishonesty, he must be willing to restore; though it is not always necessary, or even desirable, that he should give his name to the injured party. He may restore what was stolen anonymously, and sometimes the priest may assist him to do so. But care is needed lest the priest undertaking this duty is entangled in a difficulty, from which he cannot escape without breaking the seal of confession, or bringing suspicion and discredit upon himself and his office.

For example, a case is quoted in which a penitent on his deathbed entrusted to the priest a large sum of money, in order to restore it on his behalf to one from whom it had been stolen. The priest had scarcely left the house when the penitent died, and his relatives discovered that the money was missing. Suspicion fell upon the priest, who could not deny that he had taken the money, and could not explain the circumstances without breaking the seal of confession.

This is one of many difficult and peculiar cases reported in Lehmkuhl's *Casus Conscientiæ*, Gury's, and other manuals, and some acquaintance with them may be useful, but no study of casuistry will profit a man who is not gifted with common sense. Of course in the case referred to the priest should not have accepted the commission without obtaining leave from the penitent to disclose the facts, if it were necessary to protect his honour. Cases of restitution are much more complicated when the penitent is really uncertain how far he is responsible for the dishonesty of other people. Our casuistry committee has often been asked to solve such questions as these.

A shop assistant is expected by his employer to tell lies about the goods he sells; or a clerk is told to write a letter which he knows to be false; or a school teacher to make false entries in a register; and these cases are often complicated to an extraordinary degree. It is generally the duty of the confessor not to settle decisively questions in which there is real doubt, but to encourage the penitent to keep his own conscience tender, and to seek for the guidance of the Holy Spirit. Sometimes a person must be encouraged and strengthened to throw up a situation, and to run all risks, rather than to consent to falsehood and dishonesty. Sometimes penitents must be reminded that there may be factors in the case which they do not understand, and that generally it is their duty to do as they are told without seeking to judge.

It should be borne in mind that when the confessor is in doubt, he generally is able to ask advice with the penitent's consent, when there is no possibility of betraying his secrets; and the advice can be better obtained from some experienced priest than from any collection of cases.

Amongst cases of restitution must be included those in which the penitent acknowledges that he is in debt. It is sometimes the duty of the confessor to insist that the penitence is incomplete, and that he cannot give absolution, until the penitent acknowledges his obligations to his creditors and makes a definite attempt to set his affairs in order.

Of course an honest man may be in debt through no fault of his own, and may be really unable to pay. Such a one should not be refused absolution if he is willing to do his best; but if a man persists in maintaining a course of extravagant and unnecessary expenditure, while his creditors are unsatisfied, he cannot be told too plainly that he is quite unfit to communicate.

It is in cases of this sort that the whole influence of the priest should be used, not to keep ill-living people in some sort of relation with the Church, but to encourage the highest standard of honesty and truth.

Again, restitution is often due in the case of breaches of the Ninth Commandment. If a man has been guilty of lying and slandering, and injured his neighbour, not by picking his pocket, but by defaming his character, he must be shown plainly that the only reparation for a lie is to tell the truth.

It is sometimes a comparatively easy thing to tell the truth to a priest in the confessional, but much more than that is needed if a man is to recover the moral integrity which the Christian law demands. George Eliot has truly said in *Romola*.

"Under every guilty secret there is hidden a brood of guilty wishes whose unwholesome, infecting life is cherished by the darkness. The contaminating effect of deeds often lies less in the commission than in the consequent adjustment of our desires—the enlistment of our self-interest on the side of falsity—as on the other hand the purifying influence of public confession springs from the fact that by it the hope in lies is for ever swept away, and the soul recovers its noble attitude of simplicity."

From this brief summary it will appear that the cases in which absolution must be withheld are those in which the penitent is not sufficiently penitent to make restitution, or to avoid occasions of sin; but sometimes in cases of very grave sin, or of frequent relapse into sins already confessed, it may be well to delay the absolution. Sometimes a priest may well say to his penitent, "I do not doubt that you are sorry, and I am sure that God forgives you, but ought you not to prove your penitence by waiting for a while before you come to Holy Communion? Deepen your penitence by prayer and fasting, and above all by meditation on the Passion of our Lord. When you feel that you can humbly and heartily desire it and are ready for Holy Communion, come and receive your absolution." But even in the very gravest cases one would not wish to keep a penitent back for a very long period. To wait for three months or until the coming Easter should be long enough. It may sometimes be well to tell the penitent that in the Primitive Church sins like his were regarded with such abhorrence that he would have been left excommunicate for seven years, or even till the hour of his death. But that kind of discipline has been tried and failed, and the power of full and free forgiveness has proved to have infinitely greater value. It was our Lord Himself who said to a sinner, guilty of the gravest sin and brought into His Presence against her will, yet tarrying of her own accord to hear His sentence, "Go and sin no more."

It is the experience of those who have seen most of penitence that it is not severity, but tenderness, which produces the broken heart and builds up the new life on the basis of gratitude and love.

X

THE RULE OF LIFE

In an earlier chapter we saw that it is the main business of the clergy to promote holiness of life; we must not be content with merely helping people to keep clear of deadly sin. The confessional is justly discredited when it appears to be only directed to keeping sinful people in some sort of relation to the Church. It is, or it ought to be, not only the refuge of sinners but the school of saints, and in fact we find that some of the very best people look to their clergy to help them in their endeavours to live closer to God. As Dr. Pusey has said, "It is well known that when one has once tasted the 'benefits of absolution' for heavier sins, and found good for his soul in the special counsels of God's Ministers, he longs mostly to continue to open his griefs for slighter sins into which he afterwards falls; that he finds it a healthful discipline for his soul, a safeguard often by God's grace, against sin; that God gives him thereby lightness and gladness of heart, to 'go on his way' through the wilderness 'rejoicing.' Is such a one to be repelled? Is he to be told that the remedy he seeks for is only for those more deeply wounded, and bid to go into other folds, if he still would have it?"

Yes, indeed, it is a reproach to the Church of England, if it is suggested that those who ask for absolution, except under extraordinary circumstances, must look elsewhere.

It is the ministry to souls who are bent upon spiritual advance which makes the largest demand upon the patience and zeal of the clergy. If we have only a little experience of penitence ourselves, we can gladly help those who are turning to God from a life of utter carelessness and wilful sin, but how can we train saints unless we are intent, as becomes us, on advance in holiness ourselves? Happily, this does not mean that we can do nothing for those who are more advanced than ourselves. We can point to the heights beyond, if we are at least moving in the right direction. We do not claim to be a separate caste, with different ideals from the people to whom we minister. We help them most when we let them see something of our own difficulty. St. Paul is never so encouraging as when he tells us of the intensity of his own conflict with evil, as in Rom. vii. 14–24, or in 1 Cor. ix. 26, 27. A man must be in earnest if he dares to tell a struggling penitent, "I therefore so run as not uncertainly, so fight I not as beating the air; but I buffet my own body and bring it into bondage, lest by any means after that I have preached to others I myself should be rejected." It is the man who has tamed his own body and has himself well in hand, to whom penitents willingly turn; and saints will listen to the man who after years of spiritual endeavour says, "Brethren, I count not myself yet to have apprehended; but one thing I do, forgetting the things which are behind and stretching forward to the things which are before, I press on toward the goal unto the prize of the high calling of God in Christ Jesus" (Phil. iii. 13).

In the previous chapter it was pointed out that one cannot absolve a person from other sins if he is not prepared to live a Christian life, and therefore one must be prepared to suggest some elementary duties, which are indeed very generally neglected, but without which there can be no Christian life worthy of the name. Much help may be given to beginners, and even to some who have professed religion for years, if the priest who ministers to them in private will suggest a rule of life. I purposely speak of "suggestion" rather than direction, for I believe the latter implies a method, which is bad for both penitent and priest. Our business is not to enslave the conscience, or to save a person from the trouble of thinking for himself, but to place him in such a relation to God that he will look for the continual guidance of the Holy Ghost.

But the main lines may be laid down.

(I.) Clergy who do not hear confessions, or come into intimate personal relation with souls, have no idea how much even churchgoers and occasional communicants neglect the duty of private prayer; and sometimes when prayers are said at all it means little more than the vain repetition of a form learned in childhood, which has no relation to the needs of adult life.

It is surely right to insist that the very least that is required is prayer in the morning and prayer at night. For beginners it is necessary to suggest a form, and that should be one really suited to the penitent's condition; but in many cases it is even more necessary to deliver souls from the bondage of forms and encourage freedom in the lifting up of the heart to God.

There is, of course, no limit to the help which some good people naturally desire to obtain from the priest in the matter of private prayer, if only they feel that he knows anything about it; and to prepare ourselves for this higher ministry to advancing souls calls for unceasing effort.

(II.) Again, if our penitents are to grow in grace we must teach them how to use their Bibles, or in other words, to practise meditation. Its importance may be emphasised by an incident of personal experience. Two years ago I was on a steamer between Rangoon and Singapore when I met with a Japanese Buddhist priest. He was at once disposed to make friends, and came to me every morning for instruction in Christianity, and every afternoon for instruction in chess! I cannot be sure whether he was more interested in Christianity than I was interested in Buddhism, but both of us were anxious to learn what we could of the other's religion. There were certain points of agreement, and I was much edified when my friend said, "Of course the really important part of personal religion is the practice of meditation. It is necessary not only for priests and monks like ourselves, it is needed as much by men and women in the world; it gives to soldiers and sailors courage and calmness in times of difficulty and danger." This might certainly be illustrated by the courage and good temper exhibited by the Japanese, who are largely under the influence of Buddhist ideals. The habit of communing with one's own heart is an admirable preservative against panic and ill-temper.

Of course I could heartily agree with my Buddhist friend, and I told him how some of us endeavoured to practise meditation, but I was constrained to point out the limitations of his method. The Buddhist in meditation is only communing with his own heart. The characteristic attitude of a Buddhist saint in meditation, as exhibited in the colossal Buddha at Kama Kura and in the images of Buddhist saints so common in Burma and Japan, is to be seated in an attitude of profound repose with the face directed downwards. The Buddhist saint in meditation steadily contemplates his own interior—he makes the most of his own resources, and doubtless derives from his meditation the patience and self-reliance which do something to secure calmness in danger, and which, ideally at any rate, deliver him from the tumult of the passions.

I pointed out to my friend that a Christian in meditation means much more than that. He is not looking down, and looking in, but looking up, and waiting for a message from God. This, of course, was quite alien to the Buddhist's creed, as he had no idea of a personal God from whom any message should come.

I trust this digression will be pardoned, and that it will serve to emphasise the point, that the Christian should be taught to place himself day by day in the Presence of God, with some such prayer upon his lips as this: "Speak, Lord, for Thy servant heareth."

Believing that God speaks to His people by His Word, it is impossible to exaggerate the importance of the continual attitude of listening for His Voice as we place ourselves at His Feet.

Even the poor sinner just turned from evil ways must be told that he cannot worthily communicate until he learns something of this, and our disciples who wish to advance in holiness will long to know far more than we can teach. Here we shall feel our need of some serious study of ascetic theology. A real and growing knowledge of the Bible, gained by our own meditation upon it, is the necessary foundation, and next to that the confessor must be familiar with such books as the *Imitation of Christ,* the *Spiritual Combat* by Scupoli, and Law's *Serious Call.* But we must not be surprised and disappointed if some of the penitents soon pass into a realm of spiritual experience beyond our reach. The true priest will rejoice heartily when he commends his penitent to the guidance of some more competent adviser. It would be pitiful indeed if the ties formed between priest and penitent were to hinder the advancing Christian from getting better guidance elsewhere. The average priest can only hope to be a general practitioner, who shows his wisdom and humility by referring his penitents to a specialist when the need appears; but it is of the essence of all wise dealing with souls that they should be gradually taught to rely less and less on the guidance of the priest. There comes a time when it is best to say, "Taceant omnes doctores, sileant omnes creaturæ in conspectu tuo, Tu loquere solus Domine."

(III.) Next to private prayer and meditation something must be said of the duty of public worship. It is the strength of the Roman Church that every one of her children acknowledges that it is a primary duty to go to Mass, at least on Sundays and certain days of obligation. Whatever may be said against the mechanical observance of such a rule, it must be admitted that we have suffered grievously from the absence of any clear rule, or even general custom. Our best people give more time to public worship than the Roman Catholics, and we sometimes attain to a much higher ideal of corporate worship, but amongst ourselves even good-living people are very irregular and capricious in the observance of their duty. I venture to submit that when a person comes to us, in confession or otherwise, desiring to set his life in order, we should leave him in no doubt that it is a duty to come to the Lord's Service on the Lord's Day. Whether we call it the Lord's Supper, or Holy Communion, or the Eucharist, or the Holy Mass, there is only one service which can be properly described as the Lord's Service. It is not in accordance with the true ideals of the Church to absolve a sinner if he is not prepared to come to the Lord's Service on the Lord's Day, when the opportunity is within his reach. A vague promise to receive Holy Communion once a month, or to attend some other service every Sunday, is no sufficient substitute for this elementary Christian duty, and the state of religion in England would be very different if this fact were resolutely faced, and the arrangements of our public worship put upon an intelligible basis. When once the elementary duty of obedience to our Lord's own precept about public worship is established, there is room for great variety as to what should be recommended to individuals about frequent Communions, and the use of other opportunities for prayer and praise and religious instruction.

Probably much harm is done by encouraging children and young people, and new converts generally, to attend very long services, and that much more frequently than befits their spiritual condition. When the minimum requirement is once recognised, it is better to wait patiently till growth in grace manifests itself in the growing desire for prayer and praise.

Advice is often asked about frequency of Communion, and when once a penitent is restored to the grace of God, and trying to live as a Christian should, he may well be encouraged to communicate with growing frequency. It is indeed lamentable that many of our people continue to communicate only once a month because that rule was suggested at their Confirmation in the distant past. It may have been quite a good rule to begin with, but it is a very bad rule to go on with. If the monthly Communions were real and fervent, surely there would be the wish for something more, and no instructed Churchman living the life of grace should be permanently content with anything less than Communion every Sunday and Holy Day. That will be the natural consequence of the previous rule, though there are young people and others who must be warned not to attempt weekly Communions until they have made some progress in the Christian life. If a rule is asked about confession as a normal preparation for Communion, provided that it is clearly understood that the penitent is left quite free, he may be encouraged to come once a year or before the great festivals, or even in some cases once a month, but certainly not before each Communion, provided that he is ready to come at any time without delay, if he cannot otherwise receive with a quiet conscience.

(IV.) As regards fasting and abstinence, we have none of those detailed regulations which the Roman Church imposes on her children. Days of fasting and abstinence are clearly marked in the Calendar, and ought to be announced in church, but the method of observing them is left to the individual conscience. We cannot be surprised that penitent and faithful persons ask for guidance in the matter; and subject to the ultimate authority of the Bishop, or in the absence of any guidance from him, the priest must be prepared to give counsel. Sometimes fasting must be strongly recommended as the cure for sins of the flesh. There is no doubt that entire or partial abstinence from meat reduces the force of sensual desires, but great care is needed lest the advice which is sorely needed by the average self-indulgent Englishman should be unduly pressed upon his wife and daughter. She, especially if she is young and enthusiastic, is likely enough to fast in a way which spoils her temper, injures her health, and brings the whole thing into disrepute. Here the confessor chiefly needs not rules but common sense, and the experience and sympathy which come from a real effort to bring his own flesh into subjection to the spirit. Moreover, in giving counsels about abstinence and fasting we must bear in mind that there is the question of general obedience to authority, as well as the practical advantage of self-denial.

We are thinking of the man who "humbly and heartily desires the gift" of absolution, and we must assume that in doing so he desires to submit to the doctrine and discipline of the Church. He can scarcely do this unless he accepts some personal rule about the observance of those days which the Church sets apart for a special purpose.

(V.) Almsgiving should certainly be included in a rule of life, and if the confessor is consulted on the point he must not abuse his privilege by advocating charitable objects with which he is specially concerned. Nothing is more discreditable to the ministry of absolution than the suspicion that the penitent may be induced to dispose of his money under the direction of the priest. And yet it is often an obvious duty to tell the penitent that a certain proportion of an annual income or a weekly wage should be set apart for God and the poor. Here, again, there is a danger of substituting a legal bondage for the true spirit of Christian liberality. To press the obligation of the tithe is dangerous and misleading, for the tenth part of an income, whatever was the actual amount, might in one case be a generous gift, and in another far too little. Moreover, a Christian is not justified in marking off a certain proportion of his income as due to charity, while he claims that all the rest is his to spend as he pleases. We cannot get rid of our responsibility so easily as that, for we are only stewards, accountable to God for all that we possess. In this, as in every other point of Christian endeavour, our business is not to offer definite rules, but to stimulate the conscience until it seek the guidance of the Holy Ghost.

And the matter of almsgiving widens out into the whole social question. If it is not the business of the clergy to advocate special schemes of social reform, still less is it our business to acquiesce in things as they are. Our penitents must not imagine that they can remain on good terms with our Lord and His Church, if they are not greatly concerned about the needs of the poor. Perhaps something will happen when Christian people seriously lay to heart the meaning of the social doctrine of the Sermon on the Mount, and endeavour to reproduce, at least in spirit, the state of things described in Acts v. 32–35, in order that the resources of the rich may be made available to the uttermost to meet the necessities of the poor.

XI

PUBLIC DISCIPLINE AND PRIVATE PENANCE

It does not come within the scope of this little book to discuss at any length the relation between public discipline and the private ministry of absolution, but some acquaintance with the history of their divergence is necessary in order to avoid confusion and mistakes in practice. A very clear account of the matter will be found in M. Batiffol's *Etudes d'Histoire,* which includes an essay on "Les Origines de la Penitence"; and the practical importance of the historical study is marked by the fact that one of the sessions at the Fulham Conference in 1901–2 was given up to the same subject. It must be admitted freely that nearly all references to confession in the first three, if not the first five centuries, have to do with the public restoration of the lapsed to the communion of the Church, but "from the time of Origen onwards we find frequent exhortations to sinners to confess their sins to the priest (*i.e.* the Bishop) when a guilty conscience kept them from Communion."[1]

[1] Dr. Mason, Fulham Conference Report, p. 22.

This confession appears to have been made privately to the priest, but as preliminary to a public acknowledgment and to the undergoing of a period of penance, after which absolution was publicly given. This, of course, was something very different from the private confession and private absolution, which took the place of public discipline later on.

The practice of the Catholic Church is illustrated by her treatment of the three successive schisms, Montanist, Novatianist, and Donatist. Tertullian the Montanist, who in the *De Pudicitia* held that certain sins, *e.g.* idolatry, blasphemy, murder, adultery, were irremissible, may be refuted out of his own earlier work, *De Pœnitentia*, written as a Catholic. In the later work he bases his appalling severity on 1 S. John v. 16, where he regards sin unto death as being sin which can never be forgiven.[1]

No doubt there were times when the Church refused to absolve idolatry, adultery, and murder—they were in effect reserved cases; but that did not imply that God could not and would not forgive them. They were reserved for His judgment, and until the hour of death the sinner must remain excommunicate.

[1] "Secundum hanc differentiam delictorum, pœnitentiæ quoque conditio discriminatur; alia erit quæ veniam consequi possit, in delicto scilicet remissibili, alia quæ consequi nullo modo possit in delicto scilicet irremissibili" (ii. 14–16).

Pope Callistus boldly claims that the Church has power to absolve from all sins: "Ego et mœchiæ et fornicationis delicta pœnitentia functis dimitto."

As M. Batiffol remarks, it is "piquant" to observe that Callistus in his reply to Tertullian uses the arguments which the latter had used himself in the *De Pœnitentia.* The parables of the lost sheep, the lost piece of money, and the prodigal son all suggest that there is no limit to the Divine forgiveness, and this forgiveness is ministered through the Church.

"The edict of Pope Callistus has fixed the doctrine and discipline on the power which the Church has to remit sins, which it had been believed before his time ought to be reserved to God."[1]

The second stage is marked by the Novatian crisis. In the Decian persecution many Christians lapsed, and saved their lives by a formal act of idolatry, so that there were many about whose treatment some decision was required. Moreover, the difficulty of the situation was enhanced by the value attached to the intercessions of the martyrs or confessors, who, it was claimed, had not only special influence with God to secure the pardon of others, but who were supposed to exercise in person the Church's absolving power.

Thus, as M. Batiffol puts it, "The equilibrium

[1] *Etudes d'Histoire*, p. 111.

of the Church was compromised at once by the number of the lapsed and by the interference of the 'confessores.'"

S. Cyprian forbad his priests to give communion to the lapsed on producing a ticket of communion presented to them by a martyr. He regarded that not only as a grave invasion of the prerogative of the Bishop, but as indicating a misconception of the gravity of apostasy.

A quotation from a letter to his clergy exhibits the contrast between this lax practice and his own ideal:

"For that it is a most heinous sin, which the persecution has forced them to commit, themselves know who have committed it; since our Lord and Judge has said, 'Whosoever shall confess Me before men, him will I also confess before My Father which is in heaven; but whosoever shall deny Me, him will I also deny.' And again He has said, 'All sins shall be forgiven unto the sons of men, and blasphemies; but he that shall blaspheme against the Holy Ghost shall not have forgiveness, but is guilty of eternal sin.' The blessed Apostle has also said, 'Ye cannot drink the cup of the Lord, and the cup of devils; ye cannot be partakers of the Lord's Table, and of the table of devils.' He that conceals these words from our brethren deceives them unhappy; that, whereas by undergoing due penance they might by their prayers and good works appease God as a Father and merciful, they are seduced to perish more utterly; and they who might have raised themselves again fall still lower. For whereas in lesser sins sinners do penance for an appointed time, and according to the rules of discipline come to confession (ἐξομολόγησις) and by laying on of hands of the Bishop and clergy recover the right of Communion; now while the time is unfinished and the persecution still continues, and the peace of the Church is not yet restored, they are admitted to Communion, their names are offered, and penance not yet performed, confession not yet made, the hands of the Bishops and clergy not yet laid upon them, the Eucharist is given to them."[1]

Here we have clearly marked the contrast between these irregular proceedings and the disciplinary system which S. Cyprian implies had previously prevailed at Carthage.

There ought to be a period proportionate to the gravity of the offence, during which the sinner does penance; then, and not till then, is required the public acknowledgment of the sin, which is absolved by the Bishop and clergy with laying on of hands, and this carried with it the "jus communicationis."

Without dwelling on S. Augustine's dealings with the Donatists, it is enough to say that he vindicates

[1] S. Cyprian's Epistles, xvi. 2; *Library of the Fathers*, pp. 40, 41.

the right of the Church to exercise the power of the keys. Dr. Mason at the Fulham Conference quotes his reply to Vincent. "Those who would exclude adulterers from the place of repentance acted in a wholly impious way, refusing health to the members of Christ, and taking away the keys of the Church from those who knocked, and setting themselves against the merciful patience of God."

In summing up the results of his inquiry into the practice of the fourth and fifth centuries, M. Batiffol observes that the ordinary minister of penitence is the Bishop. He is in each Church in a unique sense the Sacerdos. He is the minister of Baptism; as the valid Eucharist is the one which is celebrated by him or by his deputy, so he is the ultimate authority who determines whether or no the penitent is to be restored to Communion. It is a very interesting but difficult problem to determine how, and when, the Bishops associated simple priests with themselves in the exercise of the power of the keys. M. Batiffol finds the beginning of the practice in the *Liber Pontificalis* of Pope Simplicius,[1] in whose time three central churches in Rome were appointed as the places where special priests should deal with candidates for Baptism and Penance.

At the Fulham Conference Dr. Moberly summed up the situation in a few sentences which seem

[1] A.D. 468–483.

to have been generally accepted by the Conference:

"There is no doubt that private confession first appears in relation to public discipline. As various causes by natural operation tended towards the disuse of confession in public, private confession (no longer as a preliminary but as a substitute) claimed a larger place. This culminated in the decree of the Lateran Council of 1215, which made auricular confession obligatory, at least once a year, upon all the faithful. This is the real starting-point of the mediæval period. There is no reason to question the honesty and devoutness of purpose of those who imposed the rule. It began as a practical discipline for holiness. Speculative theological explanation did not lead up to but followed after the establishment of the practice. The whole fabric of the mediæval theology on the subject gradually grew out of, and was based upon, the assumption of the universal necessity of auricular confession."

Now the Church of England in her Prayer-book, going back behind all this, (i.) expresses a longing for the restoration of primitive discipline, (ii.) abolishes the necessity of confession for all, and (iii.) leaves room for a large use of private confession, but upon a strictly voluntary basis.

In practice it is important for the clergy to remember that they have no right to repel any from the Lord's Table without reference to the Bishop. (See the rubric at the commencement of the Communion Office.) On the Bishop, as in primitive times, lies the responsibility of excluding notorious evil livers, and determining the terms on which those who have given scandal may be restored to communion. This episcopal function may of course be delegated to the parish priest to whom is entrusted a cure of souls, but the priest cannot claim any authority to act independently of the Bishop. The private ministry to individuals who confess sin, which may or may not be open and notorious, rests on a different basis. The coming of the penitent is voluntary, and his acceptance of the decision of the priest is voluntary also. If the priest refuses absolution he cannot prevent the penitent from coming to Holy Communion if he chooses to do so. That can only be prevented by public action based on public information; but on the purely voluntary basis accepted by priest and penitent alike, there is a great need for episcopal counsel as to what terms should be imposed. Though we can put no limit to the possibilities of Divine forgiveness, it must be right to insist that certain sins are of so grave a character, that the sinner should give ample proof of his penitence before he presumes to approach the Table of the Lord.

While we entirely repudiate the whole mediæval

system of compulsion, there is room for a doctrine and practice of reserving certain cases to the Bishop —or in other words, of limiting the powers which he delegates to the priest.

For further light on the historical question of the relation between public discipline and private penance, reference should be made to the long article by M. Vacandard in the *Dictionnaire de Theologie Catholique,* edited by M. Vacant (Letouzas: Paris, 1906), and to an article by Dr. Swete in the *Journal of Theological Studies,* April 1903; and, of course, Morinus, *Commentarius Historicus de Sacramento Pœnitentiæ,* is a storehouse of information.

XII

NOTES ON SOME USEFUL BOOKS

If this little book serves its purpose of awakening the clergy to the need of confession for themselves, and for a considerable number of the souls committed to their care, some will ask for much more guidance in the matter than the present writer is able to give, and so it may be useful to add some notes on books likely to be useful. A fairly full bibliography is given in a leaflet (42, *b*) published by the Central Society of Sacred Study in April 1910. Under the head of "Pastoralia" the paper quite rightly combines Christian Ethics and Casuistry, and it is important to remember that the priest, who would be a prudent guide of souls, needs a sound knowledge of principles even more than he needs some acquaintance with the way in which they are applied to particular cases. Therefore reference is rightly made to general works such as Lecky's *History of European Morals;* Dill's *Roman Society from Nero to Aurelius;* Bigg's *The Church's Task in the Roman Empire;* and behind this must lie the continual study of Christian ethics, as exhibited in the Sermon on the Mount, the Epistle of S. James, and in many passages in S. Paul's Epistles, while familiarity with the books of Proverbs and Ecclesiasticus (including many chapters which are unfortunately omitted from the Lectionary) ought to develop in the priest the sanctified common sense which is so essential to his work.

Bishop Gore's *Lectures on the Sermon on the Mount*, Dr. Charles Robinson's *Studies in the Character of Christ*, Dr. Westcott's essay on "The Church in the World" in his *Epistles of S. John*, are of course very suggestive. Amongst patristic treatises the Central Society of Sacred Study refers to the *Apologies* of Aristides and Justin Martyr, Chrysostom's *Homilies*, &c.

To these is added Tertullian, *De Pœnitentia*, and special attention should be paid to Dr. Pusey's note, to which reference was made in Chapter II. Many of S. Augustine's works are mentioned, but two of quite inestimable value are omitted, namely, *The Confessions*, and the little treatise, *De Rudibus Catechizandis*. The former is of course familiar to every priest, who desires to be "penitent himself that he may speak to the hearts of penitents," and the latter is full of useful counsels to one who has to prepare candidates for Baptism and Confirmation.

The editors of the leaflet refer to Gregory the Great and his *Moralia super Job*, but they omit any reference to his treatise, *De Cura Pastorali.* That was a treatise which S. Augustine of Canterbury brought with him into England, and nearly 300 years later King Alfred the Great turned it into English, with the intention of sending a copy to every bishopric in his kingdom.

For the instruction of the clergy in what S. Gregory calls "Ars Artium—regimen animarum," no modern treatise can enable us to dispense with his own *Pastorale* or S. Chrysostom's *De Sacerdotio.*

Passing from the Fathers to the mediæval period, we are rightly reminded that to understand the ethics of the schoolmen it is necessary to be acquainted with the ethics of Aristotle, and in S. Thomas Aquinas "the Philosopher" exercises an authority second only to that of the Fathers and Holy Scripture.

Many of our most trusted spiritual guides owe a great debt to the University, which has given to the ethics of Aristotle a central place in its studies. While the teaching of definite Christian morals was too often neglected, the average Oxford man gained systematic instruction in the distinctions between vice and virtue, in the principles which underlie the formation of habits, from the heathen philosopher, whom Dante calls:

> "The Master of the sapient throng
> Seated amid the philosophic train.
> Him all admire, all pay him reverence due."
>
> *Inferno*, iv. 128–130, Cary's translation.

The *Secunda Secundæ* of S. Thomas Aquinas' *Summa* is the greatest systematic treatise on Christian ethics, and there are very few cases of conscience on which it does not throw light. It is well worth while to be familiar with the method of the *Summa*. Almost every conceivable question about faith and morals is clearly faced. The opposite conclusions, from which S. Thomas dissents, are first clearly stated, then comes the "contra," generally a text from Holy Scripture, or a quotation from a Father, and that is followed by the reply in which S. Thomas expresses what he believes to be the mind of the Church; and finally he gives detailed answers to the opinions which he rejects. From the *Secunda Secundæ* Bishop Paget of Oxford drew the substance of his illuminating "Essay concerning Accidie"[1] prefixed to a set of sermons called *The Spirit of Discipline*. Both the Bishop's essay and the passage in the *Summa* are of the greatest value to those, who may be often called to minister to people who suffer from weariness or sloth, and find it hard to tell where one ends and the other begins. So far as it is necessary for the priest to inquire further into questions which arise under the Seventh Commandment, he will find all that he needs under *Questio cliv., De partibus luxuriæ.*

In addition to the study of his analysis of the cardinal and theological virtues and the opposite

[1] Now published separately, price 1s. Longmans, March 1912.

vices, S. Thomas Aquinas should be consulted as a safe guide to the theory and practice of prayer, and if the confessor is called upon to advise his penitent about the "religious life" in the technical sense, he will find in this great treatise much that he ought to know. S. Thomas gives far sounder teaching about the true nature and limits of obedience, than that which is current in circles where the ideals of S. Ignatius Loyola have usurped too prominent a place. S. Thomas distinguishes very clearly between the obedience which is due from all to their natural superiors, together with the obedience rightly professed by religious "ad cumulum perfectionis," and condemns a third form of obedience which he calls "indiscreta." (See II. 2, 104, v.)

The best known of the older Roman Catholic text-books are those of Alfonso Liguori, Gury, and Gaume, whose work was translated by Dr. Pusey (omitting the treatment of the Seventh Commandment), but they should be read, if at all, with the remembrance that they are full of matter which no one ought to study unless it is very clearly his duty to do so. The *Provincial Letters* of Pascal contain the most scathing exposure of the degradation of morals, for which the doctrine of Probabilism was responsible, and no one should embark on the study of casuistry without a clear warning as to the dangers, which arise when the priest is anxious to make the practice of confession easy and attractive.

One who wishes to know the worst that can be said against the practice of confession and absolution will find it in the three large volumes of Dr. H. C. Lea on *Auricular Confession and Indulgences*, and the same author has published on the same scale a *History of the Inquisition.* He also published in 1867 two large volumes on *Sacerdotal Celibacy*, and of this a third and revised edition appeared in 1907. One cannot deny the learning of these ponderous volumes, but they betray the writer's incapacity for seeing the better side of the Catholic position. Lehmkuhl's *Moralis Theologia*, published in 1887 and dedicated to the General of the Jesuits, is a book to which reference should be made by those who wish to know how the Roman Catholics are treating some of the perplexing problems which arise out of modern social conditions, and a companion volume, *Casus Conscientiæ*, was published in 1903. It will be observed that the Roman Church is not afraid to incur a vast amount of obloquy, and alienate many, whose support would be of value, by insisting on the highest standard of purity, and by refusing to tolerate that misuse of marriage which is unhappily prevalent, and very insufficiently rebuked among ourselves.

Of even more importance than Lehmkuhl is the

Enchiridion Morale of Bucceroni, who also is a Jesuit. "It contains select decrees and definitions of the Holy See, of Œcumenical Councils, and of the Holy Roman Congregations which are of most use to professors of moral philosophy and confessors." A revised edition with the most recent decrees was published in 1905.

The C.S.S.S. leaflet refers to Schneider's *Manuale Sacerdotum*, and Rickaby's *Moral Theology* (Longmans, 5s.); and similar instructions to the young priest on hearing confessions are given in many Roman text-books, but English books are scarce indeed. Jeremy Taylor's *Ductor Dubitantium* and Bishop Sanderson's *Cases of Conscience* do not meet modern needs. Marshall's *Penitential Discipline*, published in 1717, was republished in the Library of Anglo-Catholic Theology, and is described by Bishop Gore as one of its chief glories. Skinner's *Synopsis of Moral and Ascetical Theology* is manifestly incomplete. It is merely the outline of a great work which is still waiting the arrival of its author. It was the beginning of a large scheme, as yet unrealised, to provide a manual of moral theology for the use of priests in the English Church. The unfinished preface of the author indicated the breadth of view and the sound judgment which Mr. Skinner brought to his task, but his untimely death deprived the Church of all but a fragment of the projected scheme. The late Canon T. T. Carter of Clewer, who wrote the preface in 1882, says, "Alas! the task was never completed. He had scarcely begun, in the Introduction, to use the stores of material in which he was probably richer than any other English priest. This work is sent forth in the hope that it may prove to be a precious storehouse of information, and an important guide on subjects of the utmost moment, and for which no similar help has ever been provided or even attempted among us."

The American Church has done something. Dr. Elmendorf, of the Western Theological Seminary, published in 1892 *The Elements of Mŏral Theology*, based on the *Summa Theologiæ* of S. Thomas Aquinas, which exhibits the imprimatur of many American Bishops. About the same time Dr. W. W. Webb, now Bishop of Milwaukee, published *The Cure of Souls—A Manual for the Clergy based chiefly upon English and Oriental authorities.* A second edition of this work appeared in 1910, and it is almost the only book which undertakes to give a priest of the Anglican Communion systematic guidance in the work of hearing confessions.

There is of course no lack of books explaining the doctrine of confession as it affects the laity, and there are plenty of manuals for communicants which take for granted its more or less frequent use. *The Doctrine of Confession*, by the Rev. T. T. Carter

of Clewer, first published in 1865, gives a full and careful history of the doctrine, including a chapter on the attitude of English divines since the Reformation. Amongst these it must be remembered of Richard Hooker, that if his teaching was so carefully balanced that his authority is claimed by advocates on either side, his own practice was to use confession. Amongst recent books should be mentioned *The Use of Penitence,* by Edward Churton, formerly Bishop of Nassau (Mowbrays, 1905). There are few of our Bishops who have not written more or less fully on the subjects in one or other of their charges, and though the usual attitude has been one of extreme caution, nearly all of them have admitted that there is a legitimate place for confession.

In Chapter II. quotations are given from the charges of Archbishop Temple and Bishop Wordsworth of Salisbury, and side by side with them may be placed a quotation from Dr. Drury, now Bishop of Ripon. Dr. Drury was a member of the Fulham Conference on Confession, and it is evident from his book on *Confession and Absolution,* published in the following year, that he had gained much from the interchange of views with the representatives of other schools of thought. He expresses in particular, on p. 210, his obligation to Dr. Moberly. In his concluding chapters Bishop Drury writes as follows:

"Private confession as taught by our Church is

but one expression of that freedom of pastoral intercourse, that fullest possible confidence between minister and people, which ought to be encouraged and developed, and which a false view of confession and absolution is tending too much to diminish. In that happy relationship which should exist between the pastor and his flock, the value of confession in time of need cannot be denied; but the widespread feeling that something very different from the discipline laid down in the sixteenth, and more freely urged in the succeeding century, is being introduced into our Reformed Church, has much to do with the unhappy lack of mutual confidence in pastoral relations which all good men deplore" (p. 280).

It is too much to hope that the Bishop would accept this little book as advocating only the use of confession which he desired to encourage, but I trust that there is nothing which goes beyond the claim, which has been consistently made by loyal sons of the English Church, and which has always been tolerated, if not wholly approved, by her rulers.

The Report of the Fulham Conference, to which reference has been made in Chapter XI. (Longmans, 1902), will repay careful study. At the request of the Bishop of London, excellent representatives of every phase of Anglican opinion met at Fulham under the

chairmanship of Dr. Wace. Two full days were spent considering:

1. The meaning of our Lord's words (in S. John xx. 22–23; S. Matt. xviii. 18), and their use in the Ordinal, as affecting the conception of the priesthood.
2. The practice of the Church:
   (*a*) In primitive times.
   (*b*) In the middle ages.
3. The meaning of the Anglican Formularies, and the limits of doctrine and practice which they allow.
4. Practical considerations.
   (*a*) The treatment of penitents.
   (*b*) The special training of the minister.

It was inevitable from the composition of the Conference that while many misunderstandings were removed, and some historical points cleared up, there was no agreement as to the extent to which confession should be encouraged. It may be well here to quote from the chairman's report to the Bishop (p. 110):

"On the practical question, there was a deep divergence of opinion in the Conference, some members holding that the practice of confession and absolution ought to be encouraged, as of great value for the spiritual and moral life of men and women: while others were deeply convinced that its general encouragement was most undesirable, that it should be treated as entirely exceptional, and that the highest form of Christian life and faith would dispense with it and discourage it."

This divergence sufficiently explains the fact that the Conference made little or no attempt to grapple with the two last points submitted by the Bishop. We are still waiting for any authoritative guidance from the Bishops as to the treatment of penitents, and the special training of the minister.

It would be a great advantage if a similar Conference could be held, prepared to go on where the former one left off. Assuming that there is a legitimate place for confession, surely it would be wise for the Bishops to procure for the younger clergy guidance in a matter where there are great opportunities of doing good, and great possibilities of doing harm. In the absence of authoritative guidance inspired by a spirit of loyalty to the standards of the English Church, we cannot be surprised that while the vast majority of our priests are neglecting the duty of hearing confessions, others are relying far too much on the text-books of the Roman Church. The present writer has tried to hold the balance. To some he may seem presumptuous where he differs from Lehmkuhl or Gaume, while to others he may appear to advocate a wide departure from Anglican tradition.

Finally, reference should be made to a book which, while it is the work of a Roman Catholic, is a possession to be prized by every priest, as priests and laymen alike prize the *Imitation of Christ* by Thomas à Kempis, or the *Spiritual Combat* by Laurence Scupoli. The *Memoriale vitæ Sacerdotalis* of Arvisenet was translated, and adapted for the use of English Churchmen, by Bishop Forbes of Brechin, who found it not difficult to eliminate the occasional phrases which are inconsistent with our standards. However, in the judgment of the present writer such translations and adaptations ought not be required, in the case of books to be used by intelligent and instructed people. The English priest who uses the *Memoriale* in the original, as he uses the *Imitation*, will find himself continually incited to aim at the kind of life which befits a sinner, who is called to lead others to the feet of his Redeemer. Let him read again and again the chapter "De zelo animarum," "De vigilantia Pastorali," and not least that "De confessionum auditione."

"Scientiam quære in libris per studium: sapientiam vero prudentiæ, misericordiæ et æquitatis trahe de cœlis per orationem.

. . . . . .

"O Sacerdos! O tu præsertim, qui curam habes animarum! vide et perpende qualem delictorum sarcinam super caput tuam congeris, si oves tuas ad tribunal frequenter vocare, et accedentes audire negligis; vel si audiens, sine cura, sine zelo, sine æquitate rem facis.

"Quid respondebis, quando ad tribunal meum vocatus, a me judicaberis et accusaberis ab ovibus tuis, dicentibus: Periimus, quia non habuimus hominem qui nos in piscinam projiceret?"[1]

[1] *Memoriale*, ch. 58.

Printed by BALLANTYNE, HANSON & Co.
Edinburgh & London.

CPSIA information can be obtained
at www.ICGtesting.com
Printed in the USA
BVOW04s0843131216
470643BV00015B/103/P

9 781331 662662